T0190656

"In *Young Lives, Big Ambitions*, Anne Longfield meticulously unravels the disturbing narrative of the decline in children's services over the past decade. Longfield brings to light individual stories that expose a consistent failure to provide crucial assistance to these vulnerable young individuals, ultimately leading many into the clutches of criminal exploitation, particularly by drug gangs.

Many of these young lives could have been spared from the perils of criminal exploitation, preventing permanent, and at times fatal, damage. Notably, Longfield's chapters addressing the challenges faced by young girls, both in criminal activities and prostitution, as well as their roles as cheerleaders and leaders of gangs, shed light on the gendered aspect of this issue, dispelling the misconception that it solely affects boys. [She] convincingly argues that timely support and early intervention can instigate meaningful change and offer hope to these vulnerable young people, their families, and the broader community.

Young Lives, Big Ambitions serves as a poignant call to action, emphasising the urgent need to revitalise our services for young people and dismantle the tragic spiral leading towards despair and criminality. Now more than ever is the time to break this cycle and restore optimism to the lives of those who need it most."

– CHERIE BLAIR CBE, KC

* * *

"Life is just too hard for too many children. Too many face delays for support with their mental health, live in poverty, or are groomed and exploited by criminals. Anne Longfield has given her life to supporting children, and she shines a light on how we are failing too many children and offers a blueprint for radical change. She is absolutely right; we need a bold new strategy that invests in children and prioritises their wellbeing. We must be ambitious for every child, so they thrive not just survive. This book is a must-read for every MP."

– MARK RUSSELL, CHIEF EXECUTIVE, THE CHILDREN'S SOCIETY

* * *

* * *

"Anne Longfield was an outstanding Children's Commissioner for England because she saw and listened to children who are all too often unseen, unheard, and ignored. Those in care, for instance, and those with mental health needs. Since leaving that role, she has continued to throw a spotlight on our most vulnerable young people, for instance, pointing out the damage to them caused by Covid, and the dangers of violence, grooming, exclusion, addiction, and crime. This book brings together these children's voices, analyses where and how we are failing to protect them, and gives examples of excellent practice that could, and should, be reproduced around the country. It makes the case for investing in our children, listening to them, and ensuring that care really does mean care. I hope this book will inspire us all to face the challenge of protecting and supporting young people. Our future depends on them."

– ESTHER RANTZEN

* * *

"As a boy from a mining community who, as the pits shut, saw friends and acquaintances sucked into a spiral of emotional and financial decline – some going to prison, some dying as a result – I have come to regret that Anne Longfield was not there to help others help them. But she is here now. Here with a profound vision for young people, one that represents a beacon of hope for the future of this country; one that cannot be ignored."

– JAMES MITCHINSON, EDITOR, *The Yorkshire Post*

* * *

"Anne Longfield not only shines a piercingly bright light into the dark, disturbing world of child vulnerability, neglect, exploitation, and our failure to protect our children, but also shows us a way out of what she so eloquently conveys as 'nothing short of a national emergency'.

This is a shocking, compelling, and important read. Longfield's 35 years' experience in child protection shine through, along with the curiosity and compassion that has made her the leading voice in this field.

Inside these pages are radical proposals to combat urgent problems where 'young lives are at stake'. This could be the blueprint to improving the life chances of future generations."

– JASON FARRELL, HOME EDITOR, SKY NEWS

* * *

"This book provides a clear, ambitious, and much-needed road map for any government serious about supporting vulnerable children to succeed."

– BARONESS LOUISE CASEY

* * *

"Anne Longfield is a tireless champion for children and young people. Her book makes a powerful case for changing how we support those who are most at risk of exploitation or serious violence. It shows how bringing together all of the different systems that should be there to support young people – family support, schools, mental health services, youth work – is the key to building stronger communities and supporting every young person to succeed. Those in power should read it!"

– STEVE CHALKE, FOUNDER, OASIS UK

* * *

"Exposing the crisis facing many teenagers, and setting out the road map to get young people's lives back, this book shines a spotlight on a murky and complex mix of problems, and it brings clarity and urgency to what we should do about it."

– JOSH MACALISTER, CHAIR, FOUNDATIONS

* * *

* * *

"Britain's young people have no more powerful advocate than Anne Longfield. *Young Lives, Big Ambitions* is a powerful wake-up call for political leaders and a devastating critique of inaction to date. Longfield is uniquely placed to document the failures of politics and policy and to write a manifesto for change. It should echo down the corridors of Whitehall for generations."

– CATHY NEWMAN, CHANNEL 4 NEWS

* * *

"Anne was never afraid to speak uncomfortable truth to power in her Children's Commissioner role, and in *Young Lives* she continues to be a passionate advocate for young people. There are times the stark reality of some young people's lived experiences is hard to read, but the shared examples of organisations that are already making a positive difference give us hope for the future.

Thanks for writing this difficult book, Anne. This is a must-read for those wishing to improve young lives across the country."

– VIC GODDARD (EDUCATING ESSEX), CEO, PASSMORES
CO-OPERATIVE LEARNING COMMUNITY

* * *

"Few people have done more to champion the vulnerable children who fall through the gaps in society than Anne Longfield. This is a powerful, moving, and ultimately uplifting account of young lives tragically wasted and how they can be turned around."

– RACHEL SYLVESTER, *The Times*

* * *

"Anne Longfield has for a long time been a leader in children's services, and the work she does for young people in the care sector and other areas is awe-inspiring. *Young Lives* is thought-provoking, educational, and insightful. The future of our most vulnerable young people lies between the lines and the solutions come to life within the pages. One of the most important books you will read in this sector."

– CHRIS WILD, CARE SECTOR PROFESSIONAL,
CAMPAIGNER, AND AUTHOR OF *Damaged*

* * *

"This is a book that crackles with a mixture of passion, urgency, barely contained fury, and a determination that we – the adults – do better for our children and young people. It sets out the challenges on many fronts – violence, drug culture, the absence of joined-up services – but is much more than a mere howl of rage. It is also a powerful call to action, a plea backed by a plan for a new moral mission to support young lives and renew their sense of dignity, purpose, and feeling valued."

– GEOFF BARTON, GENERAL SECRETARY, ASSOCIATION
OF SCHOOL & COLLEGE LEADERS

* * *

"Anne Longfield is a passionate campaigner and compassionate advocate for children. She digs deep behind the headlines to shine a light on young people's lives. Around one in six children are from a vulnerable family in England. That is a shocking number, too many to be viewed as being on the margins of society, but they are all too often left isolated, out of sight until something significant goes wrong. This account makes a compelling case for action beyond words, to be 'relentlessly ambitious for every child' in all that we do across society."

– JONATHAN HOPKINS, NATIONAL YOUTH POLICY ADVISER

* * *

"The reality is there aren't many people like Anne Longfield. Very few see young people and their potential the way that she does. Even fewer match her dedication and determination to instigate change at a social policy level, to bring issues of young people and their families to light often in the face of those who would rather minimise or deny the reality of what is going on in young people's lives. *Young Lives, Big Ambitions* is an incredible read, a reality check on the truth of young people and their journeys, and at the same time a reminder of what happens when there is a collective failing by agencies to act, and the knock-on effect in terms of degradation of funding support by the state and the ensuing impact it has on life outcome trajectories. More than just narratives, this book has compelling statistics and builds upon existing evidence. It is therefore beneficial, providing as much value for practitioners who work with young people and their families as it does for social policy makers, councillors, and those tasked with tough decisions on what can, and should, be done next."

– JUNIOR SMART, FOUNDER, SOS PROJECT AT ST. GILES TRUST

"*Young Lives, Big Ambitions* is a call for change that details the stark realities for some of the UK's most vulnerable children and, crucially, offers practical solutions for the future.

Anne Longfield, a former Children's Commissioner for England, is well placed to lead us through the horrors children and young people too often endure and to make a positive case for why it doesn't have to be this way.

Children murdered while in the care of the state, let down by the councils that should have protected them, the schools that should have educated them, the society that turned away from their plight. Children dragged into county lines drug selling. Young people housed in substandard, taxpayer-funded accommodation, often provided by private companies turning vast profits, and preyed upon by criminals (as we detailed in a series of reports for BBC Newsnight).

With empathy and precision, Longfield catalogues the shocking details of these children's lives and the moments that are missed to protect them.

This important, timely book argues that we should be much more ambitious for young people growing up in adversity. It makes a compelling case for why we should do better. With nurture, care, and protection, these children and young people could flourish. As a society, we owe them that."

– KATIE RAZZALL, JOURNALIST AND MEDIA EDITOR, BBC NEWS

* * *

"Anne Longfield has dedicated decades to improving children's lives. *Young Lives, Big Ambitions* distils this unique perspective and unrivalled experience into a road map of hope for believing a society can act to ensure ALL its children may flourish. Picking up stories, evidence, ideas, and a compelling framework en route, she shows how early intervention, effective support, joined-up services, and reformed 'human-centred' public services can transform thousands of vulnerable children's lives. But much more powerfully, she makes the social, economic, cultural, and moral case as to why we must start the journey to reach the destination where every child thrives."

– PAUL LINDLEY OBE, FOUNDER, ELLA'S KITCHEN, BRITISH ENTREPRENEUR, AND CHILDREN'S WELFARE CAMPAIGNER

* * *

"There is no advocate for children as fierce and committed, or as knowledgeable and loving, as Anne Longfield. This book reveals the cracks in our state through which children fall into lives of county lines, crime, lost hope, and early graves. It is an urgent appeal for politicians to get their act together and make every child matter. Longfield has produced a manifesto for a revolution to end our collective failure to protect the children who need our help the most."

* * *

"In her new book *Young Lives, Big Ambitions*, Anne Longfield CBE paints a harrowing picture of the country our young people are growing up in. But, Anne also gives us hope, telling us what has to change and how – giving leaders the tools and ideas to improve young people's lives."

* * *

YOUNG LIVES, BIG AMBITIONS

of related interest

Unseen Lives
The Hidden World of Modern Slavery
Kate Garbers
ISBN 978 1 78592 635 8
eISBN 978 1 78592 636 5

Black Again
Losing and Reclaiming My Racial Identity
LaTonya Summers
ISBN 978 1 83997 318 5
eISBN 978 1 83997 319 2

Transgressive
A Trans Woman on Gender, Feminism, and Politics
Rachel Anne Williams
ISBN 978 1 78592 647 1
eISBN 978 1 78592 648 8
Audiobook ISBN 978 1 78775 309 9

Anything for My Child
Making Impossible Decisions for Medically Complex Children
Stephanie Nimmo
ISBN 978 1 80501 027 2
eISBN 978 1 80501 028 9

Young Lives, Big Ambitions

Transforming Life Chances for Vulnerable Children and Teens

Anne Longfield
With Jo Green

Jessica Kingsley Publishers
London and Philadelphia

First published in Great Britain in 2024 by Jessica Kingsley Publishers
An imprint of John Murray Press

1

A CIP catalogue record for this title is available from the British Library
and the Library of Congress

ISBN 978 1 83997 280 5
eISBN 978 1 83997 281 2

Printed and bound in Great Britain by TJ Books Ltd

Jessica Kingsley Publishers' policy is to use papers that are natural,
renewable and recyclable products and made from wood grown
in sustainable forests. The logging and manufacturing processes
are expected to conform to the environmental regulations
of the country of origin.

Jessica Kingsley Publishers
Carmelite House
50 Victoria Embankment
London EC4Y 0DZ

www.jkp.com

John Murray Press
Part of Hodder & Stoughton Ltd
An Hachette Company

Contents

CHAPTER 1

These Are Young Lives

Jaden and Jacob died within four months of each other in the first few months of 2019. Jaden was 14 years old when he was repeatedly stabbed to death. Jacob was 16 years old when he was found intoxicated and distressed in his bedroom.

They were two teenagers full of potential who should have had their whole lives ahead of them. They should have been preparing to make their mark on the world as adults. Instead, their short lives, and the multiple failures of systems that were supposed to keep them safe, are chronicled in two separate Serious Case Reviews into their deaths, both of which concluded that they had been criminally exploited. The pages of those inquiries record the ways in which many parents' worst fears can unfold and leave us with little doubt that these were two deaths that could have been prevented.

In the Serious Case Review into Jaden's death, he is known simply as 'Child C', though of course this is not how he is remembered by those who knew him and loved him. Talking about Jaden after his death, his mum described him as a 'loving baby boy...a mummy's boy who would often cling to his mother'.[1] As an older child, she remembered him as a 'loyal friend' who had plans to travel

---

1   Serious Case Review: Child C: a 14 year old boy, 2020, Waltham Forest Safeguarding Children Board.

the world and who gave out scarves and woolly hats that he'd paid for out of his own pocket to homeless people. Before he became drawn into a world of drugs and violent gangs, he had been in the top set at school, and he had loved fixing up bikes.[2] Jaden's Serious Case Review says he was 'a polite and articulate boy with considerable social skills'.[3]

In the review into his death, Jacob is described as a cheeky, determined, and friendly boy who took pride in his appearance. His family recall his kindness and his sense of humour. Professionals who knew him share memories of a child with aspirations. Yet Jacob's review also describes how he was expelled before he had even started secondary school and how he had been in trouble with the police.

Like Jaden, Jacob was groomed by criminal gangs into selling drugs in his mid-teens. His death left, in the words of the review into his death, a 'family torn apart and left heartbroken by what happened to a much-loved son, brother, grandson and uncle'. His family told those examining the causes of his death that they wanted his story to be told to influence and affect change across the safeguarding system in the UK.[4]

At first sight, the backgrounds of Jaden and Jacob look quite different.

Jaden lived in London, in the borough of Waltham Forest, one of the most diverse and, until very recently, most deprived parts of the country.

In contrast, Jacob lived in Banbury, a historic Oxfordshire market town on the edge of the Cotswolds and the heart of Middle

---

2   *Ibid.*

3   *Ibid.*

4   'Untouchable worlds': protecting children who are criminally exploited and harmed: Child Safeguarding Practice Review: Jacob, 2021, Oxfordshire Safeguarding Children Board.

England, though a place not without its share of deprivation, poverty, and crime.

In fact, these two young boys had much in common. Their tragic deaths were the end of a similar tragic journey that saw them both sucked into a dangerous criminal environment that no one seemed able to save them from. They fell through gaps in the school, care, and youth justice systems, and by the time practitioners were fully involved, they were unable to prevent tragedy from occurring.

Most of us remember what it feels like to be 14. We remember our times with friends, our experiences at school, starting to go places, and trying out new things. Our worlds are opening up, and we are trying to work out where we fit in.

Yet at the time of his murder, Jaden's life in London bore little resemblance to that of most teenagers his own age. He was homeless, out of school, and three months before he was killed, he was found with an older boy in Bournemouth, a hundred miles from home, carrying nine wraps of crack cocaine, a mobile phone, and over £300 in cash.

Yet incredibly, following his release by police, no contact was made with either Jaden's school to inform them of the arrest or with the child exploitation team in his local authority. Shortly afterwards, he was excluded from school, and in the months before his death he had spent just three of the previous 22 months in school. Half of his time out of school was while he was the subject of 'Elective Home Education' – where children are withdrawn from the school roll to be educated at home.

Jaden was out of the school system and out of contact with his teachers and peer group. Indeed, his Serious Case Review says 'In Child C's case, the current arrangements governing home education contributed to his vulnerability to criminal exploitation.'

Similarly, Jacob is described in his Serious Case Review as 'not on any school roll at any education provision…[he] was a child missing education for 22 months. Jacob's mandatory need for education was not provided by Oxfordshire County Council when he lived at home and when he was in the care of the local authority'. Four educational settings were asked to take Jacob, yet he remained off the school roll for two years. His situation was considered by education panels and his needs were monitored by professionals, including a Virtual School, a statutory service designed to support children placed in care or previously looked after in their schools.

But still nothing happened. His case was never escalated to the Education Skills and Funding Agency – the organisation that handles complaints against academies and free schools – as it should have been.

Both boys experienced more horrors in their brief teenage years than most of us could ever comprehend in a lifetime. Jacob was reported missing more than 20 times, initially from home and then his care placement. Shortly before his death, he owned three mobile phones, he was seen selling drugs, and he was recorded as a suspect or an offender in 26 police reports, mostly for violent crimes. He was even treated for knife injuries to his hands and face.

Like Jacob, Jaden had run away from home in the past and he was living with a grandparent while his mum was sleeping on friends' sofas. He became involved with the criminal justice system when he was found guilty of carrying an imitation firearm.

But it didn't need to be like this.

The two separate Serious Case Reviews into the deaths of Jaden and Jacob both show that with better help and support their lives could have been so different. Their two different reports contain many similarities, including the failure to find 'reachable moments' when their lives may have been saved.

These 'reachable moments' were the opportunities when the right interventions by the right people at the right time could have begun to change the direction of their lives.

A new set of adults – an inspirational teacher, a sports coach, a family friend – might have started to build trusted relationships with them to open up opportunities and divert them away from those who groomed them into drug dealing and violence.

In my decades of working with children and young people, I have heard and read so many terrible accounts of young lives lost or wasted, and so often there was a reachable moment that was missed.

For Jaden, it was said in his Serious Case Review to be his Bournemouth arrest, while for Jacob, it was when his knife injuries were discovered. For both boys, those reachable moments were repeatedly missed. Their families, friends, and communities are now left with only their memories and many 'what ifs'. These two vulnerable boys ended up as newspaper headlines and, in Jaden's case, identified by a single capital letter in a Serious Case Review, because they were not given the right support at the right moments earlier in life before everything started to spin out of control.

While both children were supported by numerous different professionals and practitioners in the latter part of their lives – and indeed their families talk about the dedication of many of those who tried to help – in the end, the safeguarding systems did not prevent their deaths.

We need to ask ourselves, why this is happening so often?

Why are we continuing to lose thousands of young people – mostly boys – to the criminal justice system or to life-changing acts of violence?

It is so obvious to anyone that neither Jaden nor Jacob were evil criminal masterminds. They didn't set out on this path with a grand plan. Rather, they were sucked into situations that overwhelmed them. Nobody was able to catch them.

Both Serious Case Reviews tell us that they are victims of what is technically referred to as a 'system failure'. That is true. But fundamentally, both boys were scared children, who underneath the bravado just wanted help to be normal and to be like other children.

It is heartbreaking to learn from his Serious Case Review that Jacob was 'frustrated that he had nothing to do in the day' and that he had even talked to a friend about buying a school uniform and walking into school, just to feel like the other children. But at the same time, he felt he couldn't. As his Serious Case Review says, Jacob had 'become trapped in a world he could not escape, having been coerced and controlled for many months by organised criminals operating County Lines'.

Similarly, the 'appropriate adult' who sat in on Jaden's police interview in Bournemouth said he appeared to be 'a vulnerable young person frightened by what he was being groomed and coerced into by others', giving the impression that he 'definitely wanted to find a way out of the mess he was getting into'.

Before they died, both Jaden and Jacob's situations should not have been a surprise to the swarms of professionals and services around their lives. These were not children who were unknown to the services that are there to help protect children from harm.

At the time of Jaden's death, he had five different caseworkers and plans were in place for Alternative Provision (AP) to get him back into education. AP is education arranged by local authorities for children who, because of exclusion, illness, or other reasons, would not otherwise receive suitable education. It includes education arranged by schools for pupils on fixed-term exclusions and pupils being directed by schools to off-site provision to, in the Department for Education's description, 'improve their behaviour'.[5]

Jacob had been taken into care.

Yet in both cases these interventions to change the direction of their lives, and to protect them from harm, never happened.

Jaden and Jacob were already in the same danger zone that many thousands of other children currently inhabit.

They may be out of school through exclusion or bureaucratic indifference, or on the edge of social services and statutory intervention.

They may be growing up in families where there are deep-rooted problems with addiction, serious mental health problems, domestic violence, homelessness, or poverty, or a combination of these vulnerabilities.

They may be living in inappropriate care accommodation, with little support from children's social services, at risk from those who are so good at spotting vulnerable teens to exploit.

Jaden and Jacob are two of the most tragic recent cases, but there are so many more children at risk of harm and uncertainty.

Ayoub Majdouline was 19 at the time he was convicted in December 2019 of murdering Jaden. Ayoub had previously been classified by the National Crime Agency (NCA) as a 'modern slave' after he was seen in Hampshire with a known drug dealer. The NCA was concerned he was 'being groomed by more sophisticated offenders'.[6] He had been removed from his mother's care because his stepfather abused him but was then abused again in his next home. He later went missing from various foster care placements. Ayoub was well known to children's social services and had drug and knife-carrying convictions as a younger teenager.

---

5   Alternative Provision: Statutory guidance for local authorities, 2013, Department for Education.

6   'Modern slave', 19, convicted of murder of Jaden Moodie, 14, 2019, The Guardian.

He is now serving a life sentence in prison for murder.[7]

We should all be aware of what is happening to some children today. We all have a level of responsibility to do something about it.

Whether you are developing policy, work in children's services or your local community, or are reading this book as someone who cares about the welfare of children in society, we are all capable of making an impact.

We know there are millions of vulnerable children who need extra support if they are to enter adulthood with the best opportunities to do well. We know too that within this large cohort there are those who are extremely vulnerable. These are the children who too often end up lost to gangs or sexually exploited, caught up in the criminal justice system in their teens, in care for their own protection, and leaving school without qualifications or many options. They are over-represented in our adult prisons, and are more likely to be homeless and to suffer health problems.

It is these children who need us – as individuals, and as a society – to build a protective ring of steel around them. They have a right to expect that as a society we will invest in their futures, just as we do for millions of other children who grow up without these potentially life-changing challenges. This book aims to put forward a case, with practical measures, for how we can do it.

About this book

I have worked with children for over 35 years, from providing family support in some of the most challenging parts of the country, to setting up and running a network of Sure Start Centres. I spent six years as the Children's Commissioner for England, giving a

---

7   Ayoub Majdouline jailed for murder of 14-year-old Jaden Moodie, 2019, The Guardian.

voice to children and young people in the corridors of power. Most recently I have been the chair of the Commission on Young Lives, a national independent inquiry looking at how we can improve the support and opportunities we give to marginalised teenagers.

Without a doubt, my early experiences of working with children and families in east and south-west London not only influenced me at the time but have also stayed with me ever since.

In these communities, I saw families – usually women – who were achieving wonderful things with the basics of some support in place.

These were women who were bringing up children often alone, often without much money, but with decent jobs, their own housing and friendships, and a support network on hand. With affordable flexible childcare, and additional support when needed, these families were able to flourish and grow, safe in the knowledge that they had stability of support and trusted people to turn to.

In other circumstances, these families may have been seen as 'problem families' – they were, in fact, very far from that. They worked hard and despite hardships and setbacks were determined to help their families get on. When things went wrong support was there, and it made all the difference. They were an inspiration, and they have always stuck with me.

This first-hand understanding of the difference that stable and reliable support can play has been at the heart of my work from that day on – but it has sometimes felt very out of reach in this country. On a visit to Sweden in the early 1990s, I was bowled over by the community projects for children and their families we found in large urban housing estates. Walking through the sprawling estates in the late afternoon, the winter darkness was interspersed with noisy beacons of light coming out of children's schemes every few hundred yards. It wasn't really remarked upon; it was just seen as part of life.

In this country, a decade later, it was great to see new Sure Start schemes and children's centres doing much the same in some of our own communities – sympathetically designed with spacious and light indoor space opening out to gardens and outdoor play areas for children in some of our poorest communities. These centres invited parents in, encouraging them to take part in drop-in activities, building relationships and friendships, and offering support and advice.[8]

Once again, it was clear to me that having trusted and reliable people and places to turn to could be truly transformative. Understanding the challenges and barriers children and families face and getting alongside them to offer help and support to help them flourish can be life changing.

Just like the parents in those community projects I had the privilege of experiencing in east and south-west London years ago, many parents were able to do fantastic things because they had people and support when they needed it.

That is why my starting points have always been that every child deserves the very best start in life, and where families need support to make that happen, we should make sure it is in place. That could be a little bit of help to get them back on track or specialist intervention that lasts a decade. And we should be willing to fund it properly – seeing it not as an exorbitant cost but as an investment in the future of both our young people and our country.

If the last four decades have taught me anything, it is that we have a responsibility to notice and intervene when something is going very wrong, whether that is a child at risk at home, a children's services department that is not functioning properly, or a whole system of support that is failing vulnerable children. My experience has also shown me that without people there to notice,

---

8   The health impacts of Sure Start, 2021, The Institute for Fiscal Studies.

many families are often on the edge of crisis and out of the sight of support services – until something significant goes wrong, throwing everything off course, making life even tougher. A child can then lose their way and even fall into danger, just as Jaden, Jacob, and many others did.

Over the years, I've lost count of the number of times I've heard that some children can't be helped or that we don't have evidence to know what to do. Neither is true.

When I think back to those families who I first worked with 30 years ago in different parts of London, I remember the low aspirations that were often there. A child not ending up in prison was seen as a big success. The idea that children from these families could go to university or into a great apprenticeship was seen as completely unrealistic.

We have made progress since then, with more children who live in the most deprived parts of London going on to higher education or into good jobs than during the 1980s or 1990s.[9] So much of this success is due to a more positive ambition for more children as the world has opened to education, information, travel, and culture in a way that we could never have imagined even a few decades ago.

So, when I hear the same kind of naysaying now – that gangs and criminal exploitation are problems that we can tackle around the edges but never defeat, that there is always going to be a conveyor belt of vulnerable children like Jaden and Jacob for ruthless criminal organisations to groom – I do not accept it.

This tendency to write off these families, and these children, as if they cannot ever be helped needs to be challenged every day. I have heard 'Their problems are too complex,' 'There will always be people like that,' 'It is too expensive' or even 'It's a waste of

---

9   Poor pupils in London outstrip rich in rest of country, 2014, BBC News.

time.' Often most frustrating of all are those in Westminster and Whitehall who claim that 'There just isn't the evidence available to solve it.' As Children's Commissioner during the years 2015–2021, I heard it and I sensed it in the body language of many politicians and officials. They seemed far happier focusing on the easy policy wins than on tackling the tough generational problems that are marginalising many thousands of children year after year.

The children and families I worked with 30 years ago had some of the worst outcomes, and often they weren't even on the radar of those services that could help them. We are so much better now at identifying children who are being harmed or whose families have hit crisis point, but as a society we are still providing little or nothing to many children who are not seen as vulnerable enough on one indicator or another to get automatic help – even though the problems they are living with make their lives fragile.

In this book, I hope to share with you why I believe that providing help and support for children and their families early, when problems are emerging, is the best way of reshaping our thinking on how to protect and support vulnerable children. I'll show how it can be done – in our schools, health services, public services, and communities.

I want to encourage us all to reimagine our aspirations and ambitions for all children, to consider not just systemic and political solutions but also practical steps we can take in our everyday lives that will do more to prevent children like Jaden and Jacob from ending up in crisis and instead build good lives.

I believe we can do this.

We should remember the words of Jaden Moodie's aunt, Tesfa Green. Speaking after the conviction of Jaden's murderer, she said:

My family radiate love. We adored Jaden. I could give you a list longer than my arm of our attempts to safeguard Jaden. Like when my sister painstakingly home-schooled him in Nottingham, when he went to Jamaica to spend the summer with his dad so he could be a safe distance away from exploitative adults, when my sister was begging for support from children's services.[10]

Nor can I forget how Jacob's grandfather described the appalling way he believed his grandson was treated:

> You buy a new car; you get to know it and you look after it to begin with. After a while it loses its shine and appeal and you do not have the same level of interest in it. This is what happened to Jacob, when the system did not know what else to do, the focus was lost on helping him.[11]

Jaden and Jacob were loved, and they are missed. Like many other marginalised teenagers who have ended up hurt or killed, or in prison for harming others, their young lives and their adult lives could have been so different had there been reachable moments that prevented them from becoming involved in crime or exploitation and which kept them safe.

This is what I will set out to design in this book: a vision for a society in which all young people are able to flourish and succeed.

---

10 From the collapse of a happy family to a brutal death: how Jaden Moodie was failed, 2019, The Guardian.
11 Untouchable worlds': protecting children who are criminally exploited and harmed: Child Safeguarding Practice Review: Jacob, 2021, Oxfordshire Safeguarding Children Board.

CHAPTER 2

Protecting Our Children

Jacob and Jaden were victims of the epidemic of drug-running, grooming, and serious youth violence happening right now across our country. For them, and thousands of other children, harmful criminal exploitation is sadly an ever-present reality of their childhood. This is an industry that involves tens of thousands of marginalised and vulnerable young people, which brings misery and destroys lives and prospects.

Sonny is 17 and he has a criminal record after he stabbed another teenager following a territorial dispute over drug dealing.

I met Sonny's headteacher while he was awaiting sentencing. He is a model of what a good community-minded headteacher should be. He fights for all the children in his care. He does all he can to keep every young person in school, and he provides support and advice to vulnerable families.

Yet despite his best efforts, and the brilliant team of teachers and support staff he employs in his school, Sonny still fell through the gaps.

Sonny has had a tough childhood. His mum suffers from substance misuse problems and home life was chaotic. Sonny missed a lot of school, not helped by the disruption of Covid. Staff at his school had serious concerns about what was going on at home. Although Sonny was referred to social services for assessment on numerous occasions, he did not receive any sustained intervention.

When he was eventually taken into care, he was back home very shortly afterwards. The threat to Sonny's welfare did not quite meet the high thresholds in place to manage the high demands placed on his overstretched local authority.

Sadly, this is not uncommon given so many children's services departments are financially under-resourced. Some children are sent back into the family home and relationships can understandably become even more strained than they were before they were taken into care.

Sonny stopped going to school but wanted to escape from the chaos at home, so he spent his time hanging around the streets and parks in his neighbourhood. It wasn't long before he was spotted by members of a local gang, who took Sonny under their wing. Over a period of a few weeks, they groomed him. For the first time, Sonny felt valued and important. He was being listened to by these boys. They said they would protect him and look out for him.

By now, Sonny was completely beyond his Mum's control. He had some money of his own, and he felt liked and respected. He didn't understand that he was being exploited.

But it wasn't long before Sonny was told by the boys who he had thought were his friends that he now owed the gang money. The cash and trainers that he thought were gifts turned out not to be free after all. It was now time for Sonny to pay back the gang back by dealing drugs.

Sonny felt scared and he started carrying a knife – he felt safer with it. Within weeks, he had used it on another teenage boy.

Sonny is another victim of the epidemic of drug-running, grooming, and serious youth violence happening right now across our country.

Statistics published towards the end of the Covid pandemic in 2021 revealed that almost 13,000 children in England were identified by social services as being involved with gangs.[1] In 2018/19, there were more than 18,700 suspected victims of child sexual exploitation identified by local authorities. It is estimated around 200,000 young people are at risk of serious violence, often through criminal exploitation.[2]

So, this is not a minor problem affecting only a few hundred children living in inner-city London. The police say it is now something that is being dealt with by every force in the country.

There was a staggering 124% increase in social care assessments identifying concerns about children's gang involvement between 2016/17 and 2019/20.[3]

Yet in 2019, The Children's Society published a survey showing how almost two thirds of local authorities did not have, and were not developing, a strategy to tackle child criminal exploitation or county lines.[4] Most police forces and local authorities were not even able to share the number of children affected by criminal exploitation in their area. Very few areas were collecting or providing this vitally important data. While those who exploit children are nimble and on the forefront of technology and methodology that furthers their business model, many areas aren't even sure who is at risk of becoming involved in gangs or county lines.

---

1   Characteristics of children in need: 2020 to 2021, 2021, Department for Education.
2   Violence and vulnerability: insights report, 2021, Crest.
3   Still not safe, 2021, Children's Commissioner.
4   Counting lives: responding to children who are criminally exploited, 2019, The Children's Society.

This failure to grasp the extent of the problem of county lines has happened even though the model of exploitation is now a very familiar and recognisable aspect of organised crime. It is a problem that we know stretches right across the country, from our biggest cities to small rural villages. Organised criminal networks have been exporting illegal drugs into different areas using dedicated mobile phone lines, social media, or other forms of 'deal line' for years now.

We know this county lines model relies on finding and exploiting children and vulnerable adults to move and store the drugs and money, and that they will often use extreme coercion, intimidation, violence, and weapons.

We know too how this ruthless exploitation of children happens – the promises of attention, gifts, and even love and protection. Exploiters target those who are most vulnerable, for whatever reason. Police say some of those living in children's homes are most at risk, along with young people who are missing from home, struggling with mental health problems, isolated, or out of mainstream education.

The methods used to groom them are tried and tested, and effective, and the potential for those involved in child criminal exploitation to control young people while avoiding risk themselves is enabled time and again by system failures and a business model that, like any other successful business, can identify opportunities – a failing care system, exclusion from school – and adapt quickly to changing circumstances and technological advances.

Gangs and criminals also know they need to run constant recruitment programmes to replace those who are arrested, imprisoned, or harmed, or who manage to walk away. Teenagers, and even children under 12, remain an important asset for delivering or holding drugs, and exploiters are willing to invest time and effort to achieve their aims. This can mean months of grooming, sometimes starting with the most innocuous incidents – a stranger's offer of a portion of chips in a fast-food shop – or with free drugs with the promise of more to come.

We know that once involved, children are meticulously controlled and then often retained through a debt bond, one of the most ruthless and hideous methods used by the criminals who exploit young people. The child is given responsibility for drugs and/or money and then robbed by people in the gang they don't know, and so left in debt for the goods they have lost. From this point on, they are under the control of the gang until they have paid it off. Errands are performed, including drug delivery, and commands are given to inflict violence on others.

Refusal can result in threats of violence to them and their family. I have even heard of young people being forced to pressure their grandmothers into becoming drug mules, the idea being that the police are less likely to be suspicious about or stop an older woman holding illegal substances.

These are desperate, terrifying situations for a teenager to be trapped in, and often it feels to them like there is no escape short of death or prison.

The difficult truth though is that these gangs or groups can be extremely attractive to some young people. They want to belong to something, to feel affiliated to someone or a group of people. Sometimes they are looking for relationships that are not there at home or at school. What can start as 'friendships' can, over time, fall into a different relationship, where money is offered alongside what can feel like love and support but is really manipulation.

These children are victims, just as those teenagers who were sexually exploited in Rotherham[5] and other towns and cities over

---

5   For more information see: Independent inquiry into child sexual exploitation in Rotherham (1997–2013), Rotherham Metropolitan Borough Council.

many decades are victims, and I think our response should be the same. Thankfully, the view that teenagers involved in criminal or sexual exploitation somehow 'brought it on themselves' or 'knew what they were doing' is becoming slowly extinct, though sadly, it took the horrors of large-scale sexual exploitation to change the minds of some professionals whose job it was to protect children.

Today, there is a much wider understanding about how control, grooming, and exploitation of teenagers is extrafamilial abuse – abuse by those outside the family network – and how there is often an overlap between criminal and sexual exploitation. We are also now more aware that sexual exploitation does not only affect girls, and that criminal exploitation does not affect just boys.[6]

In 2022, a crime gang that coached and exploited teenage girls into a UK-wide shoplifting scam was convicted of modern slavery offences. The girls were recruited via social media platforms or approached on the streets, trained, and transported around the country to commit fraud in high street stores using fake receipts. The conspiracy made at least half a million pounds in two years. The girls were around 14 years old and were paid for their crimes and given rewards like takeaways. In some cases, the girls were abandoned miles from home. At the trial, the jury heard how the teenagers were selected because they were vulnerable, with difficult backgrounds or mental health problems.[7]

The National Crime Agency has estimated that one in ten young people involved in county lines are girls,[8] but the Commission on Young Lives, working with Manchester Metropolitan University put estimates much higher, suggesting that as many as a

---

6   Not just a girl thing: a large-scale comparison of male and female users of child sexual exploitation services in the UK, 2014, Barnardo's.
7   Crime gang who tasked vulnerable girls with UK-wide shoplifting spree convicted of modern slavery offences, 2022, The Crown Prosecution Service.
8   NAC(19)095 County lines drug supply vulnerability and harm 2018, 2019, National Crime Agency.

third of young people in gangs are girls.[9] This could mean 60,000 girls and young women are at risk of serious violence, many of them in and around gangs. They are often recruited as they are believed to be less likely to attract the attention of police – so called 'clean skins' – and like boys, they face the same terrible physical violence, but also sexual assault.

The horrific consequences of gang violence on boys are played out regularly on our streets and in the news. But look a little closer and it is clear that thousands of girls are also being harmed, sexually assaulted, raped, or controlled in a way and on a scale that is not yet being fully recognised.

Sadly, the experiences of vulnerable girls and young women are often hidden – out of sight and out of mind – with most of the services and support to tackle serious violence, county lines, and exploitation focusing on boys.

I've heard how young men are often treated in one way, and young women in another. Young women arriving at A&E with mental health crises caused by traumatic experiences are less likely to be asked what is going on in their lives than a boy who arrives having been stabbed. They often don't feel able to talk about what is happening to them. They don't want to approach anyone for support because they are scared and feel unsafe. They can feel ashamed to talk about being abused or exploited. Every day they are suffering in silence.

If we don't recognise the prevalence of violence and control experienced by some vulnerable girls and young women, it will remain unseen and undetected, with devastating effects.

While the number of children – boys and girls – involved in gangs, criminal, and sexual exploitation in this country is

---

9   Keeping girls and young women safe: protecting and supporting the girls and young women at risk of exploitation, violence, gangs and harm, n.d., Commission on Young Lives.

shocking, it is likely to be just the tip of the iceberg. The children who appear in statistics are the ones we know about. Many vulnerable young people stay off the radar, and we know that referrals to social services from schools dropped during lockdown.

We do know that there are many thousands of young people who are growing up surrounded by addiction issues, domestic violence, serious parental mental ill health, or poverty. We know too that frequently they go unsupported and invisible to the agencies who should be able to protect them. They are the children most likely to fall through gaps in the education or care systems, and who can end up exploited by the ruthless organised criminals or abusers who have such a talent for spotting the most vulnerable.

We need to better understand the risks these young people can face outside the home too.

A 'contextual safeguarding approach' is becoming much more widespread.

The understanding of contextual safeguarding, developed by Dr Carlene Firmin, is now a recognised part of children's services' approach. It gives us a valuable understanding of the harms outside the family that can impact on vulnerable children, recognising that different relationships that young people form in their neighbourhoods, in schools, and online can feature violence and abuse. Indeed, parents and family can have little or no influence over some of these contexts and sometimes it breaks parent-child relationships.

If we understand the contextual risks that teenagers are facing, or may face in the future, and act on what these risks reveal, we should be better able to adapt the way safeguarding systems work.

When I was Children's Commissioner for England, I wanted to shine a spotlight on the experiences of these and many other groups of children invisibly experiencing harm. My office developed an annual estimation of the number of children growing up with high levels of risk. What this exposed was how an over-whelming majority of vulnerable children are neither in care nor receiving any help at all. The risks these children face rarely form overnight. For most, it will have been clear that they and their families have been struggling for some time and that they needed help earlier. Disproportionately, they are teenagers who are grow-ing up in poverty, living in areas of deprivation, and often they are from Minoritised Ethnic backgrounds.[10]

This failure to provide support at the right time for children who can end up in danger will be a strong underlying theme throughout this book. It is linked to the shrinking of systems of support that were developed in the late 1990s and early 2000s, such as Sure Start and other early intervention packages, that have been cut or allowed to wither over a decade of austerity. Even when we know that teenagers face acute risks, and we know they are vulnerable, often there is now nothing there to support them or their families.

I've worked with many children who are growing up in ex-tremely challenging circumstances, and I know that many chil-dren can be extraordinarily resilient, but we can't expect them to not be adversely affected by some of the things that they see and that happen to them.

In the year before the Covid pandemic, there were around 100,000 teenagers receiving high-cost statutory support, ranging from being in care to being on a child protection plan, receiv-ing an Education, Health and Care Plan (EHCP) or being enrolled in a Pupil Referral Unit (PRU).[11] There are also thousands more with additional needs who risk falling through the gaps, includ-ing children who receive multiple referrals to children's services

---

10   Childhood vulnerability in England 2019, Children's Commissioner.
11   Teenagers falling through the gaps, 2020, Children's Commissioner.

for support but who aren't assessed as having complex *enough* needs to require a long-term coordinated plan, children with special educational needs (SEN) or a disability, children with multiple exclusions from school, and children who are permanently excluded from school but are not allocated a place in specialist good AP.

In fact, it is estimated that before Covid around 2.3 million children in England were living with risk due to vulnerable family backgrounds. This included around 100,000 children where there was domestic abuse, parental drug and alcohol dependency, and severe mental health problems all in the same household. Prior to the pandemic, nearly 50,000 children were taken into care because of abuse or neglect at home.[12]

In 2019, of those 2.3 million children, around 669,000 were being helped through the Supporting Families Programme, a scheme providing support for families that was previously known as the Troubled Families Programme, or through various forms of children's social care. Every year, around 128,000 children are in the care system or on a child protection plan. Yet over 800,0000 of those 2.3 million were not known to or not getting support from services, while a further 761,000 were known to services but it is unclear whether they were receiving any support at all.[13]

So, in England alone, even before the Covid pandemic, around 1.6 million children from a vulnerable family were not receiving support, or if they were, it was very patchy. That is around one in eight children in England. For some of these children, life can be precarious, and it is not surprising that some of these children go on to fall off the radar and become involved in exploitation, serious violence, and the criminal justice system. There has been

---

12   Childhood vulnerability in England 2019, Children's Commissioner.
13   *Ibid.*

no national estimate of childhood vulnerability since the Covid pandemic.

A review published in 2019 of 60 vulnerable teenagers in Croydon carried out by the Croydon Safeguarding Children Board found that they had experienced multiple adversities: parental absence, drug use, domestic abuse, and poor mental health in their families. At least 41 of the children had received fixed-term exclusions in secondary school, and more than a quarter had faced multiple moves, living in homeless and temporary accommodation.[14]

Tragically, five of these young people had died by the time the report was completed.

Over the last 30 years, I've met vulnerable children from all sorts of backgrounds. We know – and some of the stories in this book show – that there are white middle-class children who become involved in county lines, criminal exploitation, and serious violence. But we cannot hide from the fact that vulnerable black children are disproportionately represented in the criminal justice system and in the children's social care system and are disproportionately likely to be excluded from school.

The levels of vulnerability in Minoritised Ethnic communities are deeply troubling and demand much greater attention and, most importantly, long-term action than they have received from government.

The fact is that if you're a Minoritised Ethnic child growing up in England today, your chances of living in poverty are high – more than half of black children grow up in poverty – and the likelihood you will develop mental health problems are high – children from the poorest 20% of households are four times as likely

---

14 Vulnerable adolescents thematic review, 2019, Croydon Safeguarding Children Board.

to have serious mental health difficulties by the age of 11 as those from the wealthiest 20%.[15]

Black children are also spending longer periods in care, more likely than their peers to become victims of crime, more likely to become involved in exploitation, more likely to become involved in criminalisation, and more likely to be locked up.

Indeed, as a society we should be ashamed that, and constantly questioning why, the proportion of imprisoned Minoritised Ethnic young people is almost four times the proportion of Minoritised Ethnic people in the UK population.[16] A review by the Labour MP David Lammy in 2017 provided extensive evidence of discrimination in the adult and youth justice systems, concluding that there is 'no single explanation' for the disproportionate representation of Minoritised Ethnic groups.[17]

David Lammy highlighted how the numbers of under-18s being charged for an offence and ending up in custody is falling, yet between 2010 and 2020 the number of black children arrested was rising. More than half of all children and young people held in secure training centres and Youth Offender Institutions (YOIs) are from a Minoritised Ethnic background, and four out of ten boys in secure training centres identify as being from a black or Minoritised Ethnic background.[18]

A staggering 87% of under-18s on remand in London between July and September 2021 were from a black or Minoritised Ethnic background.[19]

A review published in 2021 by Her Majesty's Inspectorate of

---

15 Inequalities in mental health: the facts, 2020, Centre for Mental Health.
16 Commission on Young Lives publishes its final report, 2022, Commission on Young Lives.
17 Lammy review: final report, 2017, Lammy, D.
18 *Ibid.*
19 Nine out of 10 children on remand in London come from BAME background, 2020, The Guardian.

Probation which looked at the experiences of black and mixed heritage boys in the criminal justice system[20] concluded that a large majority had experienced multiple adverse childhood experiences and that there were high levels of unmet need occurring before any contact with the criminal justice system had taken place. Almost a third had been victims of child criminal exploitation, and the majority had one or no previous convictions. Most of the boys had grown up in the poorest parts of England, and they had frequently been exposed to violence and family breakdown during childhood.

Black children, particularly black teenage boys but girls too, are also less likely to be seen as victims and are more likely to be viewed as offenders. This aspect of the 'adultification' of black children, where some black children are treated as older than they actually are, is deeply damaging and removes the protections that are generally in place for young people. It can also change the way some services and institutions treat black teenagers.

The case of the black teenager 'Child Q' in Hackney in 2022 illustrates how adultification can play out in black children's lives. Child Q was left traumatised after being strip-searched at school by Metropolitan Police officers while she was on her period.[21] That this took place at all is bad enough, but for it to take place in her school – a place of supposed safety – is horrendous. Other similar cases have emerged since. Not surprisingly, distrust in the police is high among many Minoritised Ethnic young people.[22]

There is plenty of research showing how black children can be

---

20 The experiences of black and mixed heritage boys in the youth justice system, 2021, HM Inspectorate of Probation.
21 Local Child Safeguarding Practice Review: Child Q, 2022, City of London & Hackney Safeguarding Children Partnership.
22 Nearly two-thirds of black children and teenagers do not trust police, figures show, 2022, Sky News.

viewed as both older and less innocent than their white peers.[23] It is not surprising that this view of black teenagers can lead to more punitive responses, both at school and in the criminal justice system, or the failure of safeguarding – as in the Child Q case and countless other examples when the welfare and protection of black teenagers is not considered in the same way it would be for their peers.

It is little wonder that many young black people and many black communities are deeply distrusting of not only the police but other services, including the education system, social services, and even the NHS. Rebuilding this trust is an integral part of how we tackle exploitation, serious violence, and lost life opportunities.

We need to start by treating these generational problems as a public health issue. Over the last 30 years I've heard too many politicians promise the public that cracking down on crime through tougher police action and a harsher criminal justice system is the solution to defeating knife crime, violence, and organised criminality. Yet this approach seems to have done little to stem the tide of vulnerable young people becoming victims of exploitation or serious violence. Only by addressing the underlying risk factors that increase the likelihood that an individual will become a victim or a perpetrator of violence will we really make progress. That means agencies working together to prevent violence.

The Scottish Violence Reduction Unit (SVRU) was founded in 2005 by Strathclyde Police with the intention of taking a very different approach to tackling violence, and it came at a time when Scotland's homicide rate was rising. It became a national unit in 2006, and it receives its funding directly from the Scottish Government.

---

23 Adultification bias within child protection and safeguarding, 2022, HM Inspectorate of Probation.

The SVRU team includes police officers, civilian staff, experts, and those with lived experience, and it works closely with health, education, social care, and other professionals.

While much of its work is responsive, it is a highly flexible team that combines multi-agency working and offers a range of different interventions. The proof of its good work is there to see in Scotland. Despite being a nation with significant drug problems, and other social ills, Scotland currently has some of the lowest numbers of recorded homicide cases for a single year since the mid-1970s. Between 2010 and 2020 there was a 35% fall.[24]

In 2019, then Prime Minister Theresa May announced her Government would introduce new legal duties on public services to work together to prevent and tackle serious violence as part of a welcome move towards taking a public health approach to tackling violent crime – something I had been campaigning for as Children's Commissioner.

The ethos behind this change of direction put treating violence as an infectious disease at its heart, calling on policymakers to look for a cure by using evidence to identify what causes violence and to find the right interventions to prevent it spreading.

Since then, the Conservative Government has spent over £100 million on Violence Reduction Units (VRUs), and although they have taken some time to get up and running, I am in no doubt that this approach – encouraging public and social services to work together to implement early interventions – is the right one.

We are now beginning to see some promising practice developing across the country.

The London VRU, supported by the Mayor of London's office, is now providing a wide range of interventions, including healthy

---

24 Homicide in Scotland 2019-20, n.d., National Statistics.

relationships programmes and work with schools to reduce exclusions and provide nurturing school environments.

It can be a surprise to people to learn that some of these programmes to prevent violence begin when children are still at primary school. I attended one session in a South Yorkshire school where children were asked what the most powerful weapon was that they could defend themselves with.

'Guns!' they cried out as the discussion got underway. But by the end, they all agreed that 'your brain is the thing that is really going to help you'. I saw how these children were being helped to understand the impact of violence – on them, their families and friends, and everyone else in their lives. They learned how to identify signs of grooming and work out how to avoid getting into difficult situations. 'Say you have to go home for tea,' they were told – anything, just find a reason and go.

Other VRUs are working in schools, raising awareness, training teachers and other professionals, and supporting trauma-informed work. In Manchester, they are working in partnership with the local authorities in the Combined Authority in an increasingly coherent and comprehensive approach with health, education, youth workers, and the police. These units are demonstrating what a focused approach to reducing violence looks like. For any government wanting to make violence reduction a priority, the VRUs have the potential to be a ready-made delivery unit in serious violence hotspot areas.

The Police, Crime, Sentencing and Courts Act 2021 introduced the Serious Violence Duty requiring that local authorities, the police, criminal justice agencies, and health authorities use evidence-based analysis of the problems associated with serious violence in their local areas and then produce and implement a strategy setting out how to respond to them.

This is a step forward and means that there should now be

coordinated local strategies to prevent and reduce serious violence.

Yet it's clear that in many areas this has been far from the case, with little funding for prevention and limited activity across government to make it happen.

The work of Children and Young People Safeguarding Boards, which are set up to coordinate local work to safeguard and promote the welfare of children, is also being hampered by the high thresholds of children's services that must be met before providing help. High thresholds are one way of rationing resources, and in practice, it means that most teenagers are not getting help until they are at risk of very significant harm.

Often that is too late.

* * *

This failure to intervene early has been a hallmark of the way we 'look after' vulnerable children in this country for too long. Our rickety children's social care system is bearing the brunt of the Conservative Government's frustrating refusal to deliver long-term policy and investment rather than short-term sticking plasters.

In its simplest form, the purpose of the care system should be twofold:

1. To safeguard very vulnerable children at risk of serious harm.
2. To provide them with the love and support they need to flourish and succeed.

Yet frequently it is failing, and the growing numbers of teenagers who are entering the care system and who are most likely to find it does not respond to their needs have become an enormous problem. In some cases, the care system malfunctions to such an extent that it is putting vulnerable young people directly in harm's way.

Of course, we should remember that most children who go into care are likely to have better outcomes than they would have had if they had not been removed from family environments where they were at risk of real harm. There are thousands of children in care who have a stable and loving home life, where they are cared for and where they are encouraged to do well at school.[25]

However, that is not the case for all children. A significant minority are being failed, and the argument for reforming the care system is irrefutable. Politicians and practitioners on all sides are agreed that the system is in desperate need of root and branch reform.

When I was Children's Commissioner, I lobbied the Johnson Government and Opposition parties to commit to a wholescale, independent review of the system in their 2019 General Election manifestos. As a result, the re-elected Conservative administration announced a year-long review, which began in spring 2021, chaired by Josh MacAlister.

The review was a crucial, once-in-a-generation chance to reform children's social care. As its final report, published in 2022, makes clear, without a dramatic reset, outcomes for children in care will remain poor, the numbers of children entering care will grow, and the costs – already becoming unsustainable and sometimes astronomical – will continue to rocket.[26]

Whatever people think about the detail of the recommendations, I think we can all agree that radical change is needed, with a much greater emphasis on early intervention and prevention.

---

25 Stability index 2020, 2020, Children's Commissioner.
26 Independent review of children's social care: final report, 2022, MacAlister, J.

It was clear from the outset that the care system isn't working well for many older children. There is often a failure to grasp the complexity of cases where children are open to numerous services, are both victims and perpetrators, and face harm from different and harder-to-manage sources. This has led to ineffective and confused responses, as well as a lack of accountability. The result is gaps and worse outcomes for many of these children.[27]

In 2020, the Government's Child Safeguarding Practice Review Panel, the body tasked with reviewing and learning from the deaths of children, published its own analysis of safeguarding teenagers at risk of criminal exploitation.[28] It found that even when local areas and practitioners know the children at risk of being drawn into criminal exploitation, many are not confident about what they can do to help them.

The review focused on 21 children from 17 areas who had died or experienced serious harm. Of the 21 children, 15 were from a black, brown, or Minoritised Ethnic background, and all were male. Incredibly, most of the children and their families were unknown to children's social care before problems around exploitation arose, despite the fact that 17 of the children had been permanently excluded from school.

The review concluded that whilst there are different approaches being taken across the country, there is little reliable evidence of what works and no central point where effective evidence is evaluated and disseminated.

At the local level, there was little information or working knowledge among safeguarding partnerships of what intervention strategies were being taken against the perpetrators of criminal

---

27 The case for change, 2021, The Independent Review of Children's Social Care (archived content: nationalarchives.gov.uk).

28 It was hard to escape: safeguarding children at risk from criminal exploitation, 2020, The Child Safeguarding Practice Review Panel.

exploitation. The panel also noted the contrast between the approaches taken by the authorities to children who are criminally exploited and to those who are sexually exploited – the latter approach being more well-established.

This analysis showed how often critical moments in a child's life, moments when a decisive response is vital and could make a difference to their long-term outcomes – those 'reachable moments' – are often missed. Even something as seismic as a permanent exclusion from school does not automatically always trigger intervention.

The Child Safeguarding Practice Review Panel set out a framework for local agencies that could provide a more comprehensive approach at the point when a child has been identified as being at risk of criminal exploitation.[29] This includes building a relationship with the child, actively engaging parents, and providing them with targeted support.

It is hard to believe that this is not already happening everywhere, but frequently it is not.

The MacAlister review, the Child Safeguarding Practice Review Panel, and the range of initiatives that are being undertaken by VRUs, charities, local authorities, some schools, and the police are all positive steps towards diverting children away from criminal activity and exploitation, keeping them safe, and supporting them to do well in education. The Youth Endowment Fund, which funds projects to find out what works, also has an important role to play in supporting and evaluating effective approaches to reduce violence.

However, no matter how encouraging individual projects might be, they are mostly either small scale, in their infancy, or held back by having to rely on short-term funding. This only takes

---

29   *Ibid.*

us so far. I believe we need a widespread change in how the social care system and other services respond to vulnerable teenagers on an everyday basis.

We have a system that is poor on identification and data sharing, poor on communication, confused, and uncoordinated, and frequently produces an inadequate response.

We have a system that is often completely failing to support families in crisis – even those where all the evidence is there to support intervention. Too many cries for help are not followed up.

Children who end up being exploited by gangs, criminals, or abusers are often those on the edge of the care system but receiving little or no support because they do not quite meet the high thresholds for statutory intervention. They are more likely to have an EHCP and to have attended a PRU or a secure home, more likely to be eligible for free school meals, and more likely than not to have SEN.

For some teenagers, the lack of support to deal with these life challenges can cause their mental health to spiral; given that we have a children's mental health service unable to cope with current demand, that does not necessarily mean they will receive any support.

We know that teenagers who have been exploited or who become caught up in the criminal justice system are more likely to experience serious mental health problems, unemployment, homelessness, and prison in adulthood.[30] Nearly a third of women in prison in the UK were in care at some point as a child. One in four homeless people were in care during their childhood.[31]

Most people who are in prison or who have been through the

---

30 The experiences of black and mixed heritage boys in the youth justice system: a thematic inspection, 2021, HM Inspectorate of Probation.

31 Homelessness prevention for care leavers, prison leavers and survivors of domestic violence, 2017, All-Party Parliamentary Group for Ending Homelessness.

criminal justice system can pinpoint a time or even a moment when their life could have taken a different course. Often this relates to neglect or abuse in childhood, but for many it is during their teenage years when something happened – an explosive moment with a family member, a bereavement, the introduction of a parent's new partner to the home – that escalated a difficult life into crisis.

Of course, most of us experience events during our teenage years that cause conflict or unwelcome change, but usually these moments are resolved with the support of family or friends before they spin out of control. However, some teenagers experience episodes in their life within contexts that make them more vulnerable, which then result in them going into care or becoming at risk of exploitation and criminalisation.

Sadly, it is this conveyor belt of vulnerable children, often on the edge of care or in care, that is the lifeblood of organised criminals and others who wish to exploit or harm them.

We need to see these children protected from harm and exploitation through early identification and long-term support for them and their families. This is more important than ever in light of the long-term trends of who is entering the care system, identified by the Independent Review of Children's Social Care and others in recent years.

Over the last decade, the number of 10–17-year-olds subject to care proceedings rose by 95%, with the number of 15-year-olds growing by 150% and 16-year-olds by 285%. A decade ago, adolescents made up fewer than one in five children involved in care proceedings. This has now risen to over a quarter.[32]

What is driving this change?

---

32 Final report, 2022, The Independent Review of Children's Social Care (archived content: nationalarchives.gov.uk).

Undoubtedly, part of it is a failure of prevention. The impact that funding cuts have had on children's social care is raised by every professional working with children I have met over the last ten years. The consequences of those cuts – and the shrinking of early intervention services – are so far-reaching that they have infected the whole children's social care system.

The cost of a residential place can now run into eye-watering amounts,[33] a proportion of which will be fuelling the profit margins of private providers. It is thought that at least 20% of income is put over to profit, with some saying that profits could be as high as 40% in some cases. Many providers are backed by private equity, some of them are based abroad, others have no track record of looking after children or indeed of having an interest in children beyond making a tidy sum.

With vast profits being diverted from children's services departments into the pockets of speculative investors and financial institutions, little is left to invest in the early intervention funding that could divert many vulnerable young people away from the care system in the first place and keep them with their families or in kinship care.

The result is a care system that is totally unfit for purpose for older children and which has many aspects that nobody starting from scratch would contemplate proposing.

We have a system now that tolerates thousands of teenagers in care being sent far away from their home area, sometimes to neighbourhoods that have high levels of crime.[34] This is not an occasional blip in the system; it is happening every day.

We are stripping vulnerable teenage children of their support

---

33 English councils pay £1m per child for places in private children's homes, 2022, The Guardian.

34 Out of harm's way: a new care system to protect vulnerable teenagers at risk of exploitation and crime, 2021, Commission on Young Lives.

networks and taking them from people they trust and rely on, leaving them feeling confused and out of place, largely because there is not the funding to provide them with a placement close to home.

It is shocking to learn that the corporate parent – an organisation like a council or a person who has special responsibilities to care for children and young people who are looked after by children's services – is sometimes actually placing these vulnerable children in danger.

Police mapping shows how many children's homes are located in high crime areas.[35] Under the Children Act 1989, accommodation provided by local authorities for children in care must be 'within the local authority's area' unless this is 'not reasonably practicable'.[36] Sadly, for thousands of children, it is 'not reasonably practicable' and they are sent off to live wherever there is a place for them, regardless of whether it is suitable.

The growing numbers of children entering care in their teens because their parents are unable to protect them has brought thousands of children into the system who require very significant levels of support and protection. Yet the system is not equipped to provide it. First, because it relies on family-based foster care, which is designed for younger children (who are much more likely to be happy in a family environment than older children, who often have more complex needs and a greater sense of independence), and second, because it relies on a diminishing number of residential places where demand outstrips supply.

When I first began working with children in the 1980s, children's homes were usually run by local authorities and charities. That has changed dramatically over the last two decades, often

---

35 'Risk map' highlights challenge of where to put children's homes, 2015, The Guardian.

36 Children Act 1989.

due to high costs and high risks. The private sector now accounts for over 80% of children's home places.

There are around 2,400 children's homes in England, and that number has grown over the last few years, along with the increase in the number of children going into care. However, there remains a shortage of places for teenagers, particularly those with the most complex needs, and provision is not spread evenly around the country. A decade of austerity in local government has exacerbated the problem.

This shortage of registered children's homes places has led to the growing use of semi-independent accommodation. These are places that provide accommodation and support but not the kind of full care every child in care should have as a right. They do not meet the criteria of a children's home and have only a basic level of inspection by Ofsted.

Supported semi-independent placements were once supposed to help transition children who had grown up in care into independent living, yet they are now being used as the main form of care for older teenagers coming into the system.

There has been an 89% rise in the number of children living in unregulated accommodation over the last decade, and at the end of March 2020 there were over 6,000 children in England living in these placements. An investigation by Sky News in 2021 found that at least 86 local authorities were using unregulated accommodation.[37] As Children's Commissioner, I was contacted regularly by teenagers in care who had been sent to live in hostels, or even tents, caravans, and, in one case, a barge on a canal.

Clearly, this kind of accommodation is completely unsuitable for a vulnerable teenager, making them even more at risk

---

37   10,000 children in care were sent to potentially unsafe places to live – including caravans, tents and barges, 2021, Sky News.

of criminal and sexual exploitation – often the very reasons they have been taken into care in the first place. The BBC's Newsnight also ran a series of reports revealing how easy it was for local criminals to target young people living in unregulated accommodation.[38] Some of it was chilling. No parent would want this for their own children, yet the corporate parent has a detached indifference to allowing it to happen to other people's children.

That is why we need an unequivocal ban on the use of unregulated accommodation for any child in care under the age of 18. While the Conservative Government has to its credit agreed to ban its use for under-17s,[39] this still leaves far too many vulnerable teenagers at risk of being placed in dangerous and unsuitable accommodation.

We also need more placements for children in the areas where they live and know people. As outlined above, there is no legislation to stop a council from placing a child out of its local authority area, and because of the shortage of children's home places in many local authorities, many teenagers are being moved around parts of the country to live in placements hundreds of miles away from their home.

I remember meeting one teenage girl who told me she had absolutely no idea where on the map of Britain she was living. Although the Government has said these 'out of area placements' should be a last resort, unless it is in the child's best interests, four in ten placements are now made outside a child's home local authority.[40]

Another teenage girl told me that she was moved to accom-

---

38 Unregulated homes: figures reveal at least 14 children died in care, 2021, BBC News.

39 Government bans unregulated accommodation for young people in care, 2023, Department for Education.

40 Out of harm's way: a new care system to protect vulnerable teenagers at risk of exploitation and crime, 2021, Commission on Young Lives.

modation in a seaside resort, miles from home, in a block of flats with a resident drug dealer who had an active interest in exploiting vulnerable children. Everyone knew this man was there, and the risks he posed, yet still young people were being sent into this dangerous situation.

The results are obvious: vulnerable children are left feeling isolated, without trusted advocates or social workers, a long way away from family and friends.

Many of these children are already dealing with significant trauma or struggling with mental health problems. To make matters worse, teenagers at risk of exploitation and perceived to be 'risky' often come bottom of the list for providers who prioritise 'easier' younger children.

Along with 'out of area placements', and a reliance on unregulated accommodation, the children's social care system itself is not providing long-term stability for many older children.

Multiple placement moves, multiple social worker changes, and multiple school moves are not uncommon for a significant number of children in care. Teenagers entering the care system aged between 13 and 16 are now those most likely to have three or more placements.[41]

The consequences are depressingly obvious: children experience feelings of loss and instability, the chance to build relationships is hampered, doing well at school becomes less likely, and mental health issues arise, all leading to greater vulnerability. While some moves can be positive, particularly when a child feels they have been listened to, the system itself is just far too unstable for many children to set down roots and thrive.

Nobody working with children in care thinks placing vulnerable teenagers in semi-independent accommodation that is rarely

---

41   *Ibid.*

checked outside their local authority is anything other than a huge risk.[42] I've even heard reports from the police about some smaller private providers with potential links to organised criminals. How bad can it get?[43]

We could hardly be making it easier for them to find young people to groom and to exploit.

The appalling case in 2021 of Itman Ismail and Omorie Nixon, who used missing children as part of the county lines network based in Devon and Cornwall, revealed the potential dangers children in care are exposed to. They were jailed for exploiting two 15-year-olds and two 16-year-olds to transport heroin and cocaine. Ismail was employed by a care group in London and had been Nixon's key worker.[44]

I have also heard horror stories of organised crime groups placing people in local authority housing departments to tip them off about where vulnerable children in care are being accommodated.

Just as the system is frequently failing teenagers entering care, so is it often not providing support to teenagers *leaving* care. While local authorities are supposed to stay in touch with care leavers and do have a statutory duty to provide transitionary support and safeguarding as young care leavers move to independent living, many do not.

One in four care leavers aged 17 have fallen off the radar of their local authority, drifting out of care with little or no support or plan. One in four care leavers find themselves homeless at 18.[45] Over the years, I have met with many care leavers and have heard repeatedly of the long-term harm that can be done by the failure

---

42   Teens in care 'abandoned to crime gangs', 2019, BBC News.
43   For example, Gangs place moles in care homes to groom children into drug dealing, 2020, The Times.
44   Couple jailed for trafficking teens to sell drugs, 2021, BBC News.
45   From care to where? Care leavers and homelessness, 2020, Step by Step.

to provide clear pathways out of care. It should be happening from the moment a child is taken into care, and the fact it is often not even considered at all by some is another example of a system that too often lives week to week, with little forward vision of the future for the children in its care.

When you consider the help that we provide to young people who are not in care to transition into adulthood, it is shameful how often care leavers suddenly need to find themselves somewhere decent to live, without much resource and often when they lack basic budgeting skills. Problems can also develop when care leavers who have been placed out of area develop new support networks but then find they need to start all over again when they reach 18 and return to their home area.

As the Independent Review of Children's Social Care argued,[46] while we are much better at recognising the harms facing vulnerable children than we once were, government and safeguarding agencies have still to find the best solutions for improving the children's social care system and responding to the needs of every vulnerable child on the edge of care needing support.

Too often, this failure to grasp complex cases, where children are involved with different services and are both victims and perpetrators, has led to ineffective and confused responses and a lack of accountability.

In short, different parts of the children's social care, justice, and health systems are responding differently to the same teenagers, which is leading to confusion, gaps in the system, and often worse outcomes for these vulnerable children.

All of this is then rocket boosted by years of chronic underinvestment, poor workforce morale, and the intervention of

---

46   Final report, 2022, The Independent Review of Children's Social Care (archived content: nationalarchives.gov.uk).

cowboys and fast-buck merchants in the unregulated provider market.

I have seen the consequences of this confused and inadequate response so often in my experience of working with children. It is grim, and it is happening because we have become ill-equipped to identify children at risk of exploitation and too reliant on only responding once crisis occurs. Even then, too often it is not clear who is responsible for responding if a child is at risk. Shamefully, sometimes the response is so inappropriate it puts a child at even greater risk of exploitation or harm.

CHAPTER 3

Getting Alongside Families

Twenty years ago, there was a growing consensus that supporting vulnerable families and communities improves life chances and in the long term saves all of society from picking up the immense costs of failure.

Over recent years though, we seem to have forgotten that families, whichever way you look at it, are some of our country's greatest assets. They're our workforce, our neighbours, and our communities, and they rear and nurture our future generations. At their best, families are a source of love, strength, protection, and resilience, as well as a vital source of practical help and advice. It is families that have the greatest impact on children's values, their learning, their safety, and their success in life.

Yet we don't always make their job of bringing up children easier. Though much vaunted in political slogans and election leaflets, the families I speak with rarely feel that they are centre stage when it comes to deciding how the world around them works. From local surgeries and advice lines to housing and support services, everyday help can be deceptively elusive for families that are leading busy lives.

Getting an endless 'office is now closed' message is infuriating for all of us, but for families that rely on services to support their day-to-day life, it can be much more serious. We haven't designed our services to be there for families, and when things get tough, it's clear to see.

There are the families who are stuck in desperate housing, crammed into bedrooms in a flat that is too small with leaking windows, living on estates and neighbourhoods too dangerous for their children to go out to play, but who can do nothing other than wait for years on the social housing bidding list.

There are the parents who are juggling work shifts day and night to bring income into the house, unable to afford childcare so passing children from pillar to post between family and friends, but still unable to make ends meet.

There are the parents who are fighting for support in school for their child with SEN who is stuck in a queue for assessment that has already taken over a year.

There are the parents who are at their wits' end as their ten-year-old child turns from a cheerful boy with lots of friends to a recluse who is depressed, cries a lot, and talks about killing himself but isn't deemed ill enough for help.

There is the mum who is struggling to get out of a violent relationship and is desperate to support her teenage children, and the parent who is shocked to find a burner phone and cash in a teenage son's bedroom and contacts the police and social services for help only to be told they don't do that sort of thing.

There are hundreds of thousands of families like this in our country – teetering on the edge of crisis, or even in it, without receiving the help they need to prevent problems from getting worse. When families need help, and most will at some point in their lives, many have told me that they feel they are on their own – struggling to get by and stuck in a situation beyond their control. Families who are struggling often say that they feel forgotten in the day to day – ignored and overlooked when they're in need of help with a crisis looming.

Ignoring the needs of families is so short-sighted. Well-supported families can take many things in their stride, but a family on the edge of crisis with no one to turn to can often find their problems overwhelming.

People often ask how it happens. How does a family get to the point of crisis? Surely, they would have known things weren't going well and sought help? How do families end up living in such bad housing? Why don't they do something about their heavy drinking? Why are their kids at such a poor school? Why don't they stop their teenager hanging round with those kids? Why don't they get a proper job? How could they possibly not have enough money to put food on the table? Why didn't they prevent such a tragedy happening?

These questions betray how little is understood about the lives of vulnerable families. No one sets out for life to be so hard, but for some, it starts that way, and for many people, problems and challenges compound. We don't do enough to help families thrive and we don't do enough to help them avoid crisis. That's why we need a new focus on them.

None of this means that we shouldn't put the needs and safety of children first. On the contrary, a focus on families means knowing when to intervene to protect children when there are signs of abuse and families can't cope just as much as it means supporting those who can to flourish. It means understanding the causes of crisis and understanding when change is possible.

We know how and why some families end up in crisis. The inquiries and Serious Case Reviews into tragedies that happen tell us, and families tell us themselves. Every family experience is different in its own way, but there is also almost a blueprint of vulnerability.

Recently, I met Adam, a bright 17-year-old in a YOI. He gave me a blow-by-blow account of where things had gone wrong for him, starting with when he was a baby.

Adam's mother had struggled with her mental health and drinking, and brought a new partner into the house, along with a new sibling, although the relationship didn't last, which in turn made their mum's depression and reliance on alcohol and drugs even greater. There were periods when Adam had to stay with an aunt when things at home got too bad – on one occasion for several weeks as Adam's mum had been badly injured in an accident.

Adam liked the primary school he went to at first, but he was soon involved in fights as he struggled to get on with other children who were making fun of his mum and bullying him. Life at school and home deteriorated over those years. He had never met his father.

The next few years were a blur. Adam's mum became too ill to care for her children, so they went to live with their grandparents permanently. When he started secondary school, it didn't go well, and Adam was excluded. He started to hang out with older kids who always had money and knew everyone.

Soon he was going missing, and his grandparents didn't know how to cope. He sofa-surfed to avoid the arguments and even slept in the park for a while.

With no school to go to, he could spend his time with his new friends who praised him and gave him a lot of money as he took on responsibilities and helped deliver things for them.

His involvement with this gang became serious when he started organising drug sales and delivery for them and managing the new children coming in. The 17-year-old's abilities had been recognised, and he was being well rewarded for the risks he was taking. Despite the fear of violence and threats, Adam felt like he belonged.

Talking to teenagers in youth custody, you are quickly struck by the similarities in their life experiences and backgrounds and the recurring themes that are woven through their short lives. So many have been caught in a blizzard of risky situations. Poor parental supervision and discipline, disorganisation and neglect, alcohol, drugs, and almost always little or no money in the household. These young people have likely grown up in complex family structures, and it is clear many have been exposed to a lot of different relationships.

Many of the teenagers I speak with find it hard to describe confidently all the people in their family – multiple aunts, uncles, cousins, new partners, new siblings, and half siblings, and how they are related to them, or to describe their own place in the family. Many were also born to a young mother with a history of negative and often abusive personal relationships and problems with drink and drugs.

One of the many consequences of young parenthood is how short a time the young parents can describe themselves as 'children' – and how quickly they are catapulted into 'adult' roles and responsibilities. Almost all young people in custody had their childhoods, as most of us would recognise them, cut short.

Alongside trauma, family breakdown, poor parenting, a lack of support, access to drink and drugs, and in some cases sexual abuse, there is little wonder that to many, their childhood seems a lifetime ago. Yet despite this, they themselves are of course still children. It's just they are children having to cope with the kinds of challenges in their lives that most adults would find daunting and overwhelming.

Standing in the reception of one YOI waiting for clearance to go in to talk with some young people, someone mentioned how anxious one 16-year-old boy was because he was awaiting the birth of his child. I asked if that is common – how many of the teenage boys here have children? About a fifth, I was told – it used to be more, she told me. It's probably gone down a bit lately, but no one knows, she said. It's not something we ask when they come here.

And there we have it. A fifth of the teenagers in that YOI – under the age of 18 – had themselves become fathers and begun their own family. Yet there was no mechanism or process in the system that was set up to recognise that, that asked or thought about doing anything about it. A new generation with its own challenges and a mountain to climb had begun, and the opportunity to offer help, advice, and support had been missed at the first opportunity.

The more conversations you have, the more you realise that there is a depressing consistency. Far too frequently, these serious problems are being missed and go unidentified, so difficulties are left to escalate, and children go without the help or protection they need until a crisis occurs.

I think of a boy called Jack I met who was also involved in criminal exploitation. His story is familiar and a template for many other vulnerable children who end up in danger. Jack's parents were homeless and living in a B&B. Both suffered from poor mental health, and what was happening at home affected Jack's development. The family, despite serious challenges at home, did not receive any help, and by the time Jack was five, his father was drinking too much. Jack was already behind his classmates and not meeting more than half of his developmental benchmarks when he started school, and he went on to fall out of school and into criminal exploitation.

The pattern is there that can alert us – if we look – and herein lies the problem. Those with the power to change things too often aren't looking, and as a result, vulnerable children and families are slipping from view. We need to start looking properly and to know what we're looking for.

Not all vulnerable children will have grown up with disadvantage, but most have, and the statistics speak for themselves. We know that growing up in a household where parents have addictions or suffer severe mental health conditions, or where there is domestic violence (or combinations of these factors), are likely to be very damaging.[1] A study of young people in Camden who received a caution or conviction in 2015 and 2016 and went on to reoffend in the subsequent 12 months found that over three quarters had experienced deprivation, a significant proportion had experienced sustained family dysfunction, and over half had experienced parental neglect.[2]

The link between poor housing and the adverse impacts on children and family life are also well established. We hear consistently about cramped accommodation, flats in poor repair on estates that are overrun with insects and sometimes rats, poor lighting and dark walkways, and no outside area. Hundreds of thousands of families are waiting for months without much hope that they will move up the list for suitable accommodation, often surviving in the kind of housing that most people would find shocking. Little wonder that the parents with four children living in a one-bedroom flat find life so hard, and that relationships deteriorate to breakdown.

Some children speak about how scared they are to be outside their flat because of a fear of neighbours who are acting in a threatening way. Others talk about seeing residents in distress, even harming themselves or taking their own lives. In some outer urban estates I have visited, there is a feeling of neglect, with boarded-up shops and abandoned play areas – untidy and bleak during

---

1   Adverse childhood experiences: what we know, what we don't know, and what should happen next, 2020, Early Intervention Foundation.

2   Risk of reoffending cohort strategic analysis, 2017, Camden Council Youth Offending Service.

the day and dangerous at night. These are not the family-friendly environments conducive to bringing up children. Some families have only temporary accommodation – with frequent moves and long journeys to school. Poor housing can so often lead to deteriorating mental health, stifles development, and can lead to problems with behaviour.

Community workers tell me how Covid lockdowns exacerbated many of these pressures for families living in cramped or overcrowded conditions, particularly where both younger children and teenagers were at home. For some teenagers, this was driving both tensions with parents to explosive levels and their desire to be away from home. During lockdown, police were most concerned about the safety of these teenagers in parks and the areas around the takeaways – especially when it became dark.

How have we allowed our public parks and play areas to often feel like dangerous wastelands?

I know of a 15-year-old boy who died recently in an unprovoked knife attack who was in a dark parkland area just by his school when he was murdered. A charity had been asking for permission from the council to redevelop the disused house in the park into a youth centre for over a decade without success. If they had succeeded, that same park could have been full of young people taking part in activities and having fun at 7pm that December evening. How different things could have been for that boy and his family.

Sadly, Covid and the lockdowns pushed many vulnerable families to their limits and dealt a strong hand to the gangs and criminals who exploit vulnerable children. They compounded the cocktail of risks that so many families struggle with, whilst removing many of the safety nets there to help. Worries about health, children's education and wellbeing, relationships, and bereavement all added pressure and stress on families already struggling, something we are likely to see the effect of for years to come, particularly during times of economic hardship. Reports of increased incidences of domestic violence were quick to come through from the police during lockdown, as one of the first worrying signs of what was happening behind some closed doors. Violence in the home continues to feature highly in some of our poorest communities and remains one of the biggest drivers of the increased number of children being taken into care.

The pandemic also dealt a big financial blow to families, as those with the most insecure income struggled to keep going. Replacing lost income during that time has been a constant struggle as families try to cope with the increased cost of living. The economic downturn post-Covid has compounded the problem.

As a well-off country, we should be ashamed that over 4 million children – one in three children – are now growing up in poverty in the UK.[3] It is a shocking figure and one that experts estimate may increase over the next few years.

Talk to any of those families struggling on such a low income and the impact on the whole family is clear. Most parents living in poverty are working – sometimes trying to hold down two or three jobs – but still unable to make ends meet. But as prices at the checkout have soared, so too has the number of families who are struggling to put food on the table. We are seeing more and more schools stepping in to provide food banks, clothing, and even washing machines.

The growing number of children going into the care system because their family is too poor to look after them also tells its own

---

3   Child poverty facts and figures, 2023, Child Poverty Action Group.

story.[4] Over half of the children who are given custodial sentences have been previously designated as a Child in Need.[5,6] The fact remains that most of the children who need help to develop and to flourish don't get enough support, and many do not get any at all. These children are also disproportionately black.[7]

Our systems of support need to do more to identify and respond to vulnerability early if we are to improve the life chances of our most disadvantaged children.

Ask most parents what they want for their children, and they will tell you that they want them to be happy, healthy, able to get on in life. They want to do the best they can in the hope their children will grow into happy and fulfilled adults. Yet as the Covid pandemic has shown us, we're not all in it together and we don't all have the assets to draw on when we bring up our children. That makes a big difference when crisis hits.

The good news is that families – even very vulnerable families – have strengths. Most obviously, they have a pervasive desire to do what is best for their children. If we can become better at building on these strengths, intervening earlier before problems become crises, and understanding risks and protective factors, then we can build stronger families, happier children, and stronger communities.

Around the country, there are some astonishing examples of

---

4   Rising child poverty linked to 10,000 more children in care, 2022, BBC News.

5   Under Section 17 of the Children Act 1989, 'a child will be considered in need if they are unlikely to achieve or maintain or to have the opportunity to achieve or maintain a reasonable standard of health or development without provision of services from the Local Authority; their health or development is likely to be significantly impaired, or further impaired, without the provision of services from the Local Authority; they have a disability'.

6   Injustice or in justice, 2020, Children's Commissioner.

7   Black children more likely to end up in care and less likely to be adopted, 2021, Voice Online.

individuals, local organisations, and charities that are helping make that difference.

Like the Parent Champions, working alongside health visitors to support new parents to develop strong attachments to their babies in the first few months of life, reducing early exposure to trauma and high levels of anxiety which affect the developing brain, particularly in those areas involved in emotions and learning.[8]

Such overwhelming stress can hardwire a fight or flight mechanism (when your body is always on the alert for potential threat and ready for 'fight or flight') in babies, which can have long-lasting consequences throughout life, affecting physical and mental health, relationships, and the ability to regulate emotions – one of the things we know drives risks in later childhood.

Good, loving relationships with caregivers underpin everything. Without care from parents that is nurturing and responsive to their needs and feelings, whatever else that we want for children will be much harder to achieve.

Local children's centres and family hubs provide a trusted source of support for parents that they can get to know over time with the support and specialist help on hand. The children's centre on the housing estate where parents are able to drop in with their toddler to play while they meet other parents can also be the start of a relationship with staff who can help work out any problems and help provide practical support with housing, mental health, addictions and domestic violence, health, childcare, and school.

---

8   Parent Champions are parent volunteers who give a few hours a week to talk to other parents about the local services available to families. Coram Family and Childcare developed the Parent Champions programme in 2007 to help marginalised or isolated parents who miss out on vital information about how to access local family services. The Parent Champions model is delivered by parents for parents, with the support of a local authority, children's centre, school, or local community organisation.

We have seen a move in some areas towards a more restorative 'whole-family' approach to extrafamilial harm – including exploitation and radicalisation – where families are seen as partners in the process. Here, professionals work with families, building long-term relationships to resolve problems and help them recover.[9]

There are family workers in schools who help with food, clothes, and even housing, and youth workers who work with families to help resolve the day-to-day challenges they are facing.

These trusted, committed individuals stand alongside families, understanding their lives, providing emotional support, helping them navigate the myriad of local services, being there for them, but also challenging them, providing the 'roll your sleeves up' practical support that we all can need.

When I've talked to families in tough circumstances, it is clear how much this support means to them.

However, for many, many families, this kind of support just isn't available.

So many parents are struggling to get the help they need to prevent problems escalating or when crisis hits – when they find a burner phone, or unexplained amounts of money, or knives in their children's bedrooms. Their teenagers suddenly start behaving very differently, spending a lot of time with an unknown group of friends or long and unpredictable periods of time away from home, or go missing, and their parents don't know what to do or where to turn.

I have heard how parents have called the police and social services desperate for help, only to be told that this kind of help wasn't available or to be given contradictory advice. Some parents describe having to become 'instant experts', cram reading

---

9   A whole family, whole picture approach, 2019, SafeLives.

guidance and reports night and day to find out who could and should be helping and searching the internet trying desperately to find out more about grooming, exploitation, and county lines and how it works.

This is a tall order for anyone, but for families already struggling on the edge of crisis, it can be just about impossible.

One parent told me how their child and family were left without support as their teenage son suffered greater and greater harm, only receiving a referral for help when he was admitted to hospital with multiple and life-threatening stab wounds.

The blank wall that can often face families when they ask for help can be a shock for those who aren't used to it.

Ben Nelson-Roux was 16 years old in April 2020 when he was found dead by his mum in a homeless hostel for adults in Harrogate, one of the leafiest and most affluent parts of England. His mum, Kate, described Ben as an exceptionally bright, interesting, funny, and compassionate boy, but also a child who struggled with mental health issues and was regularly using drugs. Over the last 18 months of his life, his relationship with Kate changed from the strong, warm, close relationship they'd had before.

Ben's parents believe their son was vulnerable to exploitation. He had attention deficit disorder, which affected his decision-making, and he had been moved out of mainstream education into an AP facility after he struggled at school. Ben was offered support from a series of social workers from the age of 12, but when his condition deteriorated, the local gang's grip on him tightened, and Ben's family were contacted by different organisations who they felt were giving them conflicting advice. Ben eventually left home, believing he would be offered a flat. Instead, he was moved into a homeless hostel for adults.

At the inquest into Ben's death, it emerged that less than a month before his death, someone was stabbed there. The local authority housing team searched in vain for more suitable accommodation, without success.[10]

Listening to these parents' experiences, you get a sense of the powerlessness they often feel. Families in this situation describe long periods of 'waiting to hear' – for good or bad news or their teenager returning home – interspersed with frenetic activity as they rapidly try to work out what can be done and try to communicate with their child, the police, and other services, while experiencing disrupted sleep, high levels of anxiety, and negative impacts on relationships.

Some have people they can talk to but, for others, their sense of shame and guilt, sometimes exacerbated by professional assumptions about their adequacy as a parent, means they do not always reach out to others for fear of further judgement.

Being passed from pillar to post with the hope of a short-term fix offered little hope to many of the families I have talked to who are facing deep-seated challenges. In fact, for some, this only deepened their existing scepticism and distrust of statutory services. Indeed, there is a very real sense in many communities that statutory services are neither available nor relevant to them. Many families in need couldn't tell you of any statutory or local authority help in their area.

For so many families struggling to get by, the intervention of

---

10 Mother who found Ben dead says his tragic story is...proof no child is beyond county lines gangs, 2023, Daily Mail Online.

the state seems to only symbolise more problems rather than fewer. Families talk about a sense of being judged as inadequate, investigated, and assessed, and – ultimately – having the prospect of having their children taken away.

Large gaps in service provision compound the fact that some groups are particularly poorly served, including children at risk of grooming, exploitation, and criminalisation. Similarly, the high thresholds for support, fuelled by a lack of adequate funding and a lack of knowledge of what services are available, compound the problem. The result is a patchwork of services that are often over-subscribed and can lack coherence.

When help is forthcoming, however welcome, it too often takes the form of a short-term intervention that does not tackle underlying problems. This is not what anyone running public services wants or sets out for. People need to know that those they turn to are there for them and will be able to offer real help.

We need a change of focus, with a greater proportion of funding going to long-term help for families.

Where there are positive family-focused organisations in place that get to know and stick with families over time, so often the picture becomes very different. Families tell me they value places they can turn to for a range of issues and that will deal with whatever problem arises, whether this is domestic abuse, substance misuse, behaviour, or just the stresses of life. What they don't like is the conveyor belt of assessments, referrals, and closed cases they often get.

One practitioner told me about a mother who was experiencing domestic violence but did not notify the child's school for fear of her children being taken into care, as the school would need to notify children's services. These factors were contributing to more serious incidents at home, which were driving her young people onto the streets.

Due to the difficulties of accessing culturally sensitive and inclusive services, black families can experience the escalation of minor problems or problems that, with some support, can be addressed – but which can cause family breakdown when they are not. For too many black families, trusting relationships with professionals rely on representation and cultural competency. Not surprisingly, young people and families are much more likely to engage with those who share or understand their ethnic background and culture.

So much of this is about building a community that supports families to get ahead but is also there for families when problems occur.

Sure Start children's centres remain one of the best-evidenced models of community support for families, improving parenting, improving access to health advice, and supporting children's early skills and development.

Much reduced over recent years, it is no wonder that so many parents bringing up a family are confused. For years they were courted and encouraged to ask for help as children's centres opened across the country. Over the last decade, they have watched as the help moved out of their local area and became more and more limited and difficult to access. Spending on early intervention support in areas of England with the highest levels of child poverty has fallen by over half over the last ten years.[11]

None of this has helped improve the lives of children and

---

11   Children in crisis: the role of public services in overcoming child vulnerability, 2021, House of Lords Public Services Committee.

families, and it has proved a false economy too, with more money spent later as costlier and higher-intensity interventions are needed.

Between 2010 and 2020, local government spending on early intervention fell by 48% to £1.8 billion, while money spent later on costlier interventions such as youth justice, looked after children's services, and safeguarding increased by 34% to £7.6 billion.[12] For some of those families I've met, the pandemic and the move to online services really put the lid on their expectation that local informal support from their local authority was something they could count on when things got tough.

The children entering secondary school this year will be a new generation of those who have grown up without a local children's centre, many of which started to dwindle as budget cuts hit from 2011 onwards. This system-wide model of providing whole-family, joined-up, family support services has already proven it can deliver family support services from pregnancy through a child's early years and later childhood, and that it can provide some support into early adulthood.

Positive improvements in parent-and-child relationships, preparedness for school, and improvements in health, and a reduction in hospitalisation are just some of the proven outcomes that demonstrate the positive impact of this work.[13]

Established and still regarded by many as a New Labour intervention, the Sure Start model remains, in my view, vital to ensuring vulnerable families have trusted people to turn to near to home with specialists on hand for support when needed. The focus by

---

12   First Report of Session 2021/22 (November 2021) Children in crisis: the role of public services in overcoming childhood vulnerabilities, 2021, House of Lords Public Services Committee.

13   Sure Start had major health benefits for children in poorer neighbourhoods, 2019, Nuffield Foundation.

the Conservative Government has been on family hubs.[14] Their extended support for 0–19-year-olds makes sense and puts a welcome spotlight on older children, although it is important to say that there are very few family hubs, scant central resources to develop them, and even less to run them.

I have always campaigned for Sure Start style support for children of all ages and their families. But the problem is the lack of resources behind Sure Start or family hubs over the last decade, which has led to a major decline in the number of centres. Where they do still exist, they often do so with only a fraction of the services and support they used to offer.

Government once invested £1.8 billion per year in Sure Start children's centres, and investment to rebuild the infrastructure of early support is widely supported by professionals and parents alike. Whatever the next government wants to call it, local, joined-up, accessible, bespoke programmes of support with trusted professionals will transform our communities, putting services alongside families who need them, with the long-term relationships needed to identify when help is required and bring agencies together to help in a joined-up way.

There are already many organisations providing incredible support to families, and it will be important to incorporate these into any new programmes of support.

I've seen at close quarters the brilliant work that the Oasis charity, founded in the mid-1980s by Steve Chalke, is doing in some of the most deprived areas in the country. Oasis runs over 50 schools, and it has developed its own Oasis Community Hub holistic model which brings schools, local partners, and families

---

14   Sure Start had a greater focus on early years help, whereas family hubs are – in theory – aimed at 0–19-year-olds. Some also offer different services to Sure Start.

together to enable young people and families to develop the skills and character to be more independent.[15]

Oasis Community Hubs actively involve community members in designing, delivering and leading activities, including youth clubs, mentoring and vulnerable family support, holiday activities, community kitchens, food-growing projects and financial inclusion.

I visited the Oasis Community Hub in Oldham and saw how positive relationships and trusted workers are at the heart of all they do. Families feel able to reach out for help when there are problems, and youth workers are able to build close relationships with young people to help keep them safe.

The hub works alongside the nearby school, supporting pupils who need some extra help and working with parents to build their skills – some of whom have taken up training and are themselves leading programmes in the centre.

The Oasis Hub in Hadley in Enfield has a team of community workers and volunteers running a variety of services, including food parcels and parental support. Oasis Academy Hadley is part of Oasis Hub Hadley, with the community centre situated just over the road from the main school building. It caters to the needs of the whole community and is clearly a trusted asset for many families and young people who are often deeply distrustful of statutory services.

Its whole approach is based on building trust and sticking with families, and it supports families to engage with those statutory services they may otherwise not engage with.

For all communities, these centres and hubs provide the basis

---

15 Oasis hosts the Commission on Young Lives, which I have chaired since September 2021, and which is developing new models to protect vulnerable children and young people and support them to succeed.

of a new phase of support for families, with the potential to build and restore the kind of help so many families need.

They make sense for families, and they also make sense financially. The Institute for Fiscal Studies has assessed this model of combining universal services with an area-based focus on disadvantaged neighbourhoods and concluded it does provide important lessons for existing services and government's approach to future such developments.[16]

It will be down to the political parties to decide what goes in their next election manifesto, but for the families I talk to, this gets their vote.

Government should also build on the Supporting Families Programme – previously called the Troubled Families Programme – which remains the largest government programme working with families facing multiple disadvantages. The most recent 2015–2020 evaluation of its work[17] showed the programme was successful in reducing the proportion of children in care and reducing the number of adults and young people receiving custodial sentences.

Over 80% of families taking part in the programme said their key worker was helpful, with this increasing to 91% for those who saw their key worker every week. Analysis shows savings of £2.28 for every pound invested.

The Conservative Government decided to double its investment in the programme in 2022 following positive evaluation. But think how much more could be achieved if the programme were really expanded and funded to join up with children's centres and family hubs so that every disadvantaged family could have help on hand. That would really begin to transform opportunities for our poorest communities. It would really be levelling up.

---

16 *Ibid.*
17 National evaluation of the Troubled Families Programme 2015–2020: findings, 2019, Ministry of Housing, Communities and Local Government.

Doing all we can to build the strength and resilience of families should be the urgent mission of every country. Helping to prevent problems developing and escalating is good for children and families and for all of us as a society.

I believe some children of all ages who are falling into crisis would not do so if their families had received help earlier or at crucial times of transition. While many of those families are those in areas of lowest income, poor housing, and underinvestment, this is not always the case, as the tragic death of the Harrogate teenager Ben mentioned earlier shows.

I met the founder of a campaign group last year. The group was set up by a parent after her teenage son was exploited into drug dealing, and it supports and advises mothers who are going through the same experience with their own child. The founder of the group found there is a high correlation between teenagers going missing from home, domestic abuse, and criminal exploitation. Her son was engaged with youth offending services and is now successfully working and supporting himself.

He told his mum that one of the reasons he became involved in drug dealing was to support her financially as a single parent.

AIM argues that children who experience adverse childhood experiences and trauma at home, such as domestic violence or upheaval, are often in a fight or flight mode.

AIM works to create trust, build more positive relationships, and include the parents' and child's voice. It works with mums when their child is at risk, reducing stigma, listening, and being there for the (usually single) parent to talk with.

AIM took off after its founder attended a community meeting after there had been attacks in response to a fatal stabbing in the area. Someone at the meeting said it was all the mothers' fault. She shared her story and invited other mothers to come and speak to her after the meeting. She was inundated. She now receives referrals from a range of services, including family services and word of mouth.

Most of this work is voluntary, and as with so many other brilliant grassroots projects, funding is often precarious. Replicating its model is tricky, because it is so hyperlocal and flexible, but AIM's values – recognising the voice of parents and families, having a trusted advocate to turn to – are universal.

The organisation SPACE (www.bespaceaware.co.uk) is a similar self-funded organisation, founded in response to the growing prevalence of child criminal exploitation and county lines. It argues for parents to be given a far greater role in safeguarding. When parents flag concerns – they know their children and recognise changes in them – they should be listened to. SPACE believes in a welfare approach to child exploitation and aims to have a much more sophisticated understanding around issues of consent, in relation not only to child sexual exploitation but county lines too.

Those who seek to exploit children know that families can get in the way, and we need to remember this when we are looking for solutions to stop them.

For the teenagers in care, we must assume this is also the case, begging the question of why there hasn't been more of an emphasis on family interventions for parents with teenagers at times of extreme crisis. Of course, some of this can be explained by the fact that so many family relationships have broken down by the time the decision to take the teenager into care is made. Months and months of grooming and exploitation as families are deliberately driven apart can often destroy relationships and parents lose the battle to keep their children safe.

But it is also a sign of the lack of experience and confidence many of those whose responsibility it is to safeguard teenagers have in working collaboratively with families at this peak time of crisis.

Experts point to a system that is risk averse and is more comfortable with taking teenagers at risk of exploitation into care and moving them away from the area than with navigating the complexity of family relationships to support the whole family to keep their teenager safe. Where they do exist, these approaches are still in their infancy, often a product of an individual's convictions and determination to make it work. Working with families with teenagers in extreme crisis is too often still seen as unusual and high risk in this country.

I have been hugely impressed by the work done by the organisation SHiFT (www.shiftuk.org). I met them in Greenwich, one of a number of boroughs they work in, where they are working closely with around 20 young people at risk of becoming involved in the criminal justice system, and their families.

Shift's 'Guides' are selected because of their skill set and experience, rather than their professional title, and they work empathetically with young people. The team includes social workers, residential care home workers, youth workers, and those who have lived experience of care and the criminal justice system.

The Guide works closely with the young person and their family for around 18 months – although they very much have an attitude of being prepared to 'stick' with a young person for as long as they're needed. They build relationships and are truly trusted.

SHiFT's emphasis is on hope and aspiration – they do whatever it takes to help families progress and support themselves. This 'going with the flow' attitude is centred on being flexible and informal, leading to families becoming more accepting of support.

These different approaches are possible and are far more commonplace in other countries. For example, in Denmark, there is a long-standing culture of working in partnership with families where additional care and safeguarding is needed. In Australia and New Zealand, kinship care is the norm, turning first to families and their networks to explore possibilities to provide care if needed.

Other countries are using the Family Group Conferencing approach, centred on family group decision-making.

More children and young people can be helped to be safely and appropriately looked after in their own 'family' networks, by bringing family, friends, and connected others together to help them understand the professional's concerns and then support the family group to come up with a supported response to those concerns.

Widely used in New Zealand and Australia, these Family Group Conferences have been adopted as a way of working in several areas of the UK over recent years.

Allowing the family group to have private family time to work out a plan that can then be signed off by the social worker is important. When I first saw these conferences in action, I was so impressed that I referred to them as 'magic meetings' – they just seem so obviously a good thing to do if the situation allows.

In Leeds, the local authority has championed this approach and says that nearly all plans drawn up by a family group are considered as good as, if not better than, anything a social worker could have come up with. They're also more likely to work. As one senior sector leader that has pursued a family focus told me, the key ingredient towards making change like this happen is having a willingness to see 'family' as the most important but most forgotten, ignored, underfunded, unrecognised, and underused utility of the 21st century – and then working to change that. I think Family Group Conferences should be built in as an entitlement for families. Imagine the difference it could make.

A shared approach to care, local children's homes, and foster arrangements so families can continue to be involved, plus edge of care support (support for children and young people who are just below the statutory threshold where they would be taken into care, and at risk of meeting the threshold) and respite and a positive approach to building family relationships beyond crisis – all in the context of the safety and protection of children – is what an ambitious and responsible care provision should be about.

So, what kind of support is needed for families to support vulnerable children and teenagers at risk?

First, help that is constant, gets alongside families, and is based on trusted relationships.

Help should come from people and professionals who understand the lives of those they are working with, who understand the impact of past traumas, and who can see and help tackle the causes of the problem as well as the problem itself.

Help should respond to problems early, when they emerge, and understand and see the dangers before they become a crisis.

We need decent housing and safe communities that have safe places for children to meet, play, and be independent as they grow up, and we need services that prioritise and work around families in need in a joint mission – particularly education, social care, crime/police, housing, and welfare – and that work closely together to share information to prevent children falling through the gaps.

We need help that builds on the strengths of families and helps them to succeed whenever that is possible.

We need political parties to put help for families at the centre of plans for government, with a national mission enshrined in legislation to help disadvantaged families succeed. That means making long-term investment in prevention and early intervention to provide families with the local support they need from pregnancy to adulthood.

It means building new centres of support for families – rolling out children and family centres and hubs in all disadvantaged areas as the centrepiece for support and coordination of agencies – including specialist support for families through an extended Supporting Families Programme.

It also means baking in a new 'family approach' to children's social care, with a new entitlement for families to be involved in decision-making about their support through a Family Group Conference when they are referred to statutory services for help.

And it means developing new models of intense family support for families and kinship care to provide intensive, culturally attuned interventions for teenagers on the edge of care so they can remain safe and with their families and developing and piloting new shared care models of social care that involve and build the strength and capacity of families as part of residential care.

We need a serious programme to tackle poverty, with a national plan from government and across government – bringing together education, health, housing, work, training, and of course the welfare programme, and led from the top. And we need to put supporting children and families at the heart of the approach to reduce and eradicate poverty.

Who now remembers that back in 2014 the then Prime Minister David Cameron planned to introduce a 'Family Test' to ensure all government policymaking was assessed for its impact on families? This proposal was lost and forgotten a long time before the tidal wave of Brexit and the pandemic came along. But it's still a good idea and, if backed up with ambitious plans to support families, and serious money, is one that any future contender to lead our country should revive and commit to reintroducing.

CHAPTER 4

Out of School and into Harm

School and college are such an important part of any child's life, the place where the world and knowledge can open up, where friendships are formed, where children learn to build and manage relationships, and where they can work out who they are and what they might want to do with their future. A good school gives options and opportunities for children to flourish. It can be a place of security, safety, and enjoyment and should be one of the cornerstones of both childhood and a strong local community.

For most children, despite a few inevitable hiccups along the way, school is a rewarding experience that ends with good grades and a chance to go to university, into training, or into a job.

We should celebrate these schools, and the important role schools and colleges play in setting up our children to succeed in life, and be proud of the great outcomes that many children achieve in our education system.

But it is not the same for all children, and we need to remember school is theirs too. They need an education and it's our duty as adults to make sure they get one.

Unfortunately, too many children, particularly vulnerable children, are falling through the gaps in education and are leaving school without the skills and qualifications that can help them to succeed. The number of children who are excluded, are home educated, or move between schools has grown significantly over the last decade. Since the pandemic, there has been a huge surge in children who are not attending school regularly, and I worry we are in danger of this becoming the new normal. We need to wake up to what this means for children – and what it means for the country's workforce and economy of the future.

It's not always possible or right to draw a straight line between a child spending time not in school to them becoming a victim of violence or being involved in crime, but it's often a warning sign, and in some cases, the link is clear to see.

Such was the case for one 15-year-old boy who tragically lost his life in 2019. Tashaûn Aird died after being stabbed in the street. He had been permanently excluded from school, and three months before his death he had been seriously injured in another stabbing incident. The Serious Case Review carried out after his death says there had been a noticeable increase in police contacts and concerns about deteriorating behaviour and escalating risk – he was going missing and local intelligence suggested he was being criminally exploited, possibly into county lines.[1]

Tashaûn's case review shows how he received two fixed-term exclusions in May and June 2017, then a third after he was said to have damaged the property of a teacher. Despite reports he was responding positively to this third sanction, he was permanently excluded by the school a few weeks before the summer holidays of July 2017. As most children broke up from school looking forward to the long summer holiday, this child left not knowing where he would end up.

If a school excludes a child, the guidance says that they

---

1   Serious Case Review: Tashaûn Aird (Child C), 2020, City of London & Hackney Safeguarding Children Partnership.

must tell their local authority without delay. This didn't happen in this case. The authority made representations to the school and challenged the permanent exclusion. A managed move[2] was suggested, as was AP, but the Serious Case Review says the school ignored this advice, and the permanent exclusion went ahead. Following an appeal by the family, the exclusion was quashed by the Independent Review Panel, and the school was directed to reconsider the permanent exclusion. But nothing changed.

Despite the finding, the permanent exclusion was upheld, and Tashaûn continued in AP.

After his death, a former teacher at the school told the Serious Case Review that the matter leading to his permanent exclusion was not so serious that it warranted a permanent exclusion. It was, they said, instigated by lobbying from other teaching staff who just wanted to see the back of Tashaûn. As a result, the boy was educated with a group of other excluded pupils, some of them with complex needs and some of them with links to gangs, criminality, and antisocial behaviour.

The Serious Case Review concluded that Tashaûn's exclusion was a 'significant incident' and a 'catalyst to the deterioration in his behaviour'. The decision 'exposed him to a new, more challenging environment that he realistically did not need', the school failed to exhaust all available opportunities to keep this teenager at his secondary school, and 'several serious concerns were ignored by the school'.

Finally, 'the school was determined to permanently exclude [him] without consideration of the wider implications to his safety, well-being or his education'.

---

2   A managed move is a voluntary agreement between a school, parent/carer, and student to change school or educational setting.

Every child has the right to expect the education system will support them and provide a good education, and Tashaûn Aird had this right too. That may sound obvious, but it's an important principle that we would all think should run through the whole education system. Positive outcomes for every child should be our ambition and should be at the heart of any successful education system.

This is particularly relevant if we are to have a society where everyone can have good life chances – the kind of inclusive society I think we should aspire to be, where everyone has a chance to succeed and is supported to do so.

Indeed, if you look around the world at the highest-performing countries and education systems, they are where the gap between those children who do well at school and those who do not is narrow. In England, after a short period where that gap did become smaller, it is now growing again.[3] That can't be right.

Our attainment gaps – the difference between what affluent and disadvantaged children achieve – are large, and our education system is still leaving behind far too many children.[4] It is also failing to stop – and in fact sometimes encouraging – thousands of children, like Tashaûn and Jacob and Jaden, from falling out of education, either temporarily or altogether, sometimes with disastrous consequences.

Surely we should judge our education system not only by the exam results of those who do well but also by what it does for those children who need extra help or who are vulnerable – those children with SEN, the children who are already struggling with

3   Permanent exclusions and suspensions in England: 2021 to 2022, 2023, Department for Education.

4   No improvement in school attainment gap in England for 20 years, report says, 2022, The Guardian.

communication or behavioural issues when they start school, the children whose families might not always see the value of education, the children who feel they don't fit in, the children with mental health problems, the children growing up in poverty, or those children who are faced with serious difficulties at home.

Sometimes it is just the child at the back of the room sitting quietly but not really engaging, watching others take part but feeling that this isn't really for children like them.

Of course, an experienced and committed teacher will understand that some children need more encouragement and support to learn and with the right environment and back up services will be able to help them succeed.

In so many great schools, these children are cherished and valued, they are supported and looked after.

Like a child I know, whose teacher made extra time for them when their dad died, talking to them and supporting them to get involved in art and writing. It helped the child understand their own feelings and made them feel valued. They won't ever forget the help their teacher gave them.

Sadly, it doesn't always work like this. High levels of need and the pressure of the system, the focus on grades as the primary measure of success, or (sometimes as a result of this) a school's less inclusive culture means that there isn't the time, bandwidth, or tolerance to look behind the difficulties that some children may be struggling with.

Sometimes parents tell us how it felt that their children were viewed as a problem that could be pushed onto someone else to deal with and largely ignored by placing them outside mainstream school.

The tactics some schools have employed when doing this are

well known – encouragement into 'home education', off-rolling (the practice of removing a pupil from the school roll without using a permanent exclusion, when the removal is primarily in the best interests of the school rather than the pupil) or exclusion, and – increasingly – managed move after managed move. We already know too that the results can be disastrous for children's prospects and sometimes their safety. Shockingly, every year, tens of thousands of children in England are either not in school or not receiving the support they need to thrive in school.

A 2019 inquiry by the teaching union Association of School and College Leaders (ASCL) pointed towards this 'forgotten third' of children – around 30% of 16-year-olds fail to secure a standard pass (Grade 4) in English and maths, limiting their life chances.[5] It is often the same kinds of children who end up in this situation year on year – usually boys who are socio-economically disadvantaged, have learning disabilities, and are of a certain ethnic background and family background.

Why haven't we noticed?

So, while we should celebrate the progress and the success of much of our education system over the last three decades, and the opportunities it provides to millions of children, we also need to admit and confront the fact that the system isn't working for thousands of others.

I believe it should be a national scandal that almost one in five teenagers leave education without basic qualifications in maths and English. We should be equally concerned that thousands of children's prospects are being hampered by factors like exclusion, persistent absence, or poor-quality AP outside mainstream schools.

---

5   The forgotten third, 2019, Association of School and College Leaders.

One teacher told me that she was given a list of 13 Alternative Providers for a child who needed some time out of his regular school, only one of which had the curriculum that would enable him to carry on studying for his GCSEs. How short-sighted and limited is this approach? The children who need some additional help in school could be some of our best teachers, engineers, social workers, and coders of the future. Many could be getting great grades too with the right help.

The consequences of a school system that does not always value inclusiveness can also go much further than just leaving school without decent grades, damaging though that can be. There will be some who fall through these gaps in the education system, putting them at greater risk of coming into harm's way.

In my view, we still permanently exclude too many children from school, and we are sometimes too quick to rely on exclusion and suspension as solutions to 'difficult children'.

Excluding a child from their school, their peer group, trusted adults, and their daily routine and structures is a tough sanction. I've met children and adults who remember being excluded, who talk about the feeling of rejection and marginalisation that exclusion can bring. They talk about how they felt cast aside, unimportant and forgotten, with little hope for their future education or their life chances.

Some teachers will say how important it is to be able to exclude children to ensure that other children are able to learn without fear or distraction. Some teachers have even told me that the only way they can ensure that children get the specialist help they need is to exclude them.

What sort of dysfunctional system have we created that is unable to provide the help needed without resort to punishment and exclusion?

Over recent years, there has been a focus on tough behaviour policies in schools that has not always been good news for many children who struggle in the classroom environment. Of course, behaviour policies are essential to keeping school a good place to be and calm, but when they become punitive and are taking a very low-tolerance approach to behaviour that removes children without asking what is causing challenging behaviour and without trying very hard to help, they can start to become very difficult and often prohibitive for some children. School can become overwhelming, particularly to those with SEN. Too many children tell me that they spend hours and days in isolation or reflection rooms staring at a wall or falling asleep. That's not what we want for any child's education, yet sadly, it's becoming far too common in some schools.

The links between school exclusion and involvement in criminal exploitation or serious violence are not straightforward, and they won't apply to most children. But there are too many educationalists who are too quick to deny that exclusion can be a significant factor in a child's involvement in the criminal justice system.[6] There is no doubt in my mind that children being out of school can put some of the most vulnerable children at great risk of harm and exploitation. When you have spoken to as many young people in custody and in crisis as I have, you are left in little doubt that being out of school can pour rocket fuel on already difficult lives and vulnerabilities.

Last year, I met Jackie, the mother of Joe, and a group of other mums. Their children were all getting good mentoring support now but had all been excluded from their primary schools

---

6   Education, children's social care and offending, 2022, Department for Education and Ministry of Justice.

over recent years. Joe was just five years old when he was suspended from school a staggering 14 times within the space of six months.

Jackie told me that this was before they had received an attention deficit hyperactivity disorder (ADHD) diagnosis for Joe. Typically, he would wreck the room he was in, and the school would call Jackie to go and get him. Often, she would only just have got home from drop-off in the morning and her phone would go and she would have to go back to school again. This was exhausting for everyone.

At first, the school dealt with it by excluding Joe for a few days. However, after one incident when he threatened to harm himself, they decided to expel him. Jackie was devastated and was constantly ringing up to try and get Joe a school place.

After a few weeks, Jackie was told that there was a place for Joe at a PRU. When they visited it, there had been an incident that day, so every door was locked behind them. Jackie thought, 'I can't send my son here, he's only five years old.' So she refused the place and Joe spent the next few months being 'home schooled'.

Eventually, another school place was found for him, and things went well at first. But Joe soon started to play up again, and over the next year he was suspended many more times for his behaviour. Jackie came to dread hearing the words, 'Can we just have a moment?'.

Finally, Jackie received a referral to the Child and Adolescent Mental Health Service and Joe had a weekly session. This was the start of a much better time, and she was able to get a job and wasn't worrying all the time. The school put in place an educational plan giving Joe one-to-one support.

However, when Joe was eight years old there was another episode at school. Jackie arrived at reception and Joe was in the reflection room with the headteacher and deputy head. He was still smashing it up when she walked in. She went to her GP in tears and asked for help, which is when Joe was diagnosed with ADHD.

Jackie hoped this would be a turning point and that Joe would receive the support he needed, but the issues at school continued. By this point, Joe was on reduced hours, which were further shortened over time. He is now hardly at school before Jackie picks him up.

She can no longer work and feels very stressed. Her relationship with the school has gone downhill. At the start she was quiet and respectful, but Jackie realised over the years that she would have to fight and be loud if she wanted to receive the support Joe needed.

'Sometimes,' she told me, 'I feel I want to scream. I'm so tired of fighting for things that he should have because of his educational plan.'

Understandably, Jackie is worried about what will happen at secondary school. Joe has already said to her, 'What if I can't get into school?'. She knows he's scared. She doesn't want them to look at his past and think about that rather than his future. Joe loves music and Jackie wants him to enjoy his education and want more for himself. She continues to look forward to the day that he can go to school and say goodbye, and she can get on with her day without worrying there will be another call from school.

The experiences of Joe and Jackie beg the question: how this could happen? What is going on in an education system that doesn't have better ways to identify and respond to a young child who is struggling with school? Why isn't the system able to provide support to some of our most vulnerable children? And what needs to be done to change that?

It is extraordinary that we are still having a debate about high numbers of exclusions and suspensions when we have known for decades that children who are excluded from school for long periods almost always do poorly at school.

It should be impossible to ignore the increases in school exclusion over the last decade and not be concerned that something in the education system is not working.

Statistics show that it is often children with special educational needs and disabilities (SEND), those from certain Minoritised Ethnic groups and poorer backgrounds, and those in care who are disproportionately excluded, and we know that excluded children are twice as likely to be in the care of the state, four times more likely to have grown up in poverty, seven times more likely to have a SEN, and ten times more likely to experience recognised mental health problems.[7]

You are much more likely to be excluded from school if you are a black boy than a white boy.[8] Indeed, the experiences of the education system of many black children are often poor. A study by Buckinghamshire New University that interviewed black and dual-heritage children using children's social care services and black social workers, found that many of the children taking part in the research felt their teachers were often 'judgemental' or 'prejudicial'.[9] Research has also found that teachers may have higher expectations of white and Asian students' academic potential, while non-black teachers can have lower expectations of black students

---

7   Making the difference: breaking the link between school exclusion and social exclusion, 2017, Institute for Public Policy Research.

8   Summer term 2021/22: permanent exclusions and suspensions in England, 2023, Department for Education.

9   How the care system is letting down black children, 2017, The Voice Online.

and are more likely to negatively judge pupils from Minoritised Ethnic backgrounds.[10]

The Centre for Research in Race and Education has also found that black students are more likely to be placed in low-ranked teaching groups, where they are less likely to experience the best teachers or to make good academic progress.[11] Neither teacher education courses nor school inspections include a mandatory section on race equality and, despite minority children making up around a third of state school rolls, the teaching workforce is more than 90% white. This is a particular problem in primary schools.

Racial bias within the school system has been raised with me by so many people over the years. Black children have told me about the low expectations of some teachers around what they could achieve, about the way they were propelled through disciplinary systems much more quickly than other children, about how they were viewed as older and less innocent than their white friends, and about how they were perceived as 'angry' in the classroom. They have said how they felt they were often disproportionately targeted by 'draconian' zero-tolerance behaviour and uniform policies in schools.

There are also deficits around the current school curriculum for Minoritised Ethnic children. It can feel outdated and partial. Being able to see and hear yourself in what you are learning can make all the difference in whether you want to be in school or not, and ultimately, in achievement. Developing a curriculum that is inclusive has to be a priority if we are to support all children to reach their potential.

Some parts of the school system have also been too quick to

10   Tackling teachers' low expectations of black Caribbean students in English schools, 2022, Demie, F.

11   The Centre for Research in Race and Education – CRRE, 2023, University of Birmingham.

label children 'troublemakers' and 'poor learners'. Her Majesty's Inspectorate of Prisons urged the Department for Education to make sure that the SEN of black and mixed heritage boys are assessed and responded to at the earliest opportunity, and to work with Ofsted to include this in its inspection framework.[12]

This is supported by many conversations I've had with children, families, community workers, and school leaders. It would be clear to see if schools were held to account for monitoring rates of racial disproportionality in the use of permanent exclusions and for taking action to tackle this.

The system should be far more interested in looking at the impact of adverse childhood experiences, racism, and personal circumstances on some black children's experiences of the education system. This is also an area that Ofsted could be doing much more to capture in its inspection framework. Both have a public service equality duty – in the words of David Lammy – to ensure academy trusts and local authorities 'explain or reform'.[13] Exclusion from school is a problem affecting teenagers more than children of any other age, though there has been a rise in primary exclusions in recent years. There are also the 'unofficial exclusions' used by some schools. Around three quarters of 'unexplained exits' from schools in 2017 were experienced by vulnerable pupils.[14]

What happens to these children who are in and out of school, or worse, out of school for long periods?

To be abundantly clear, nobody is suggesting that every single permanent exclusion or suspension from school will lead to a child becoming involved in crime or serious violence. Yet I have met so many school leaders, youth workers, social workers,

---

12 The experiences of black and mixed heritage boys in the youth justice system, 2021, HM Inspectorate of Probation.
13 The Lammy review, 2017, Lammy, D.
14 Measuring pupil inclusion in school groups, 2022, Education Policy Institute.

victims and perpetrators of exploitation, parents, and children who have recounted how school exclusion was a trigger point, and how being out of school consistently was one of the reasons why a child became more vulnerable to involvement in county lines, gangs, or criminal or sexual exploitation.

In 2021, in the London Borough of Croydon, five teenagers were murdered by other young people – all of whom had been excluded from school at the time.[15] I refuse to believe that this is just coincidental.

So, while we should not assume that every child permanently excluded or suspended from school will become involved in serious violence or criminal exploitation, neither should we dismiss the fact that some of those children do. Moreover, while some of those children will have been involved in gangs or crime before exclusion, some will not, and they will become exposed and endangered after falling through gaps in the education system.

This debate around the correlation between school exclusion and suspension and the involvement in serious violence or criminal exploitation is unlikely to be resolved any time soon. But what is not in doubt is that those in the criminal justice system are more likely than not to have been excluded from school at some point and that there are clear links between poor educational engagement and exclusion from school and involvement in crime, exploitation, violence, and gangs.

The HM Chief Inspector of Prisons for England and Wales found in its annual report for 2017–18 that 89% of detained children and young people aged 12–18 reported being excluded from school at some point.[16] The Prisoners' Education Trust reported

---

15 Vulnerable adolescents thematic review, 2019, Croydon Safeguarding Children Board.

16 Annual Report 2017–18, 2018, HM Chief Inspector of Prisons for England and Wales.

that a third of women in prison were expelled or permanently excluded from school (this compares to 1% of the national population).[17]

One study of prisoners in adult prisons in the UK found that 63% had been temporarily excluded while at school and 42% had been permanently excluded. Six in ten boys subject to court orders have been excluded from education, most of them permanently.[18]

Time and again I have heard those people who have ended up in prison or involved in the criminal justice system talk about their negative experiences of the school system. There are adults in prison now who were in trouble at school because of their behaviour in class, sometimes trigged by undiagnosed autism or other needs, who ended up in isolation or being excluded from school and became easy pickings for those who exploit children and young people. Helpfully, the Government has started to commission research looking at links between exclusion and involvement in serious violence, and research published by the Department for Education and the Ministry of Justice has looked at the education and children's social care background of 77,000 children who had been cautioned or sentenced for an offence. It found that seven out of ten children who had been cautioned or sentenced for an offence had received a school suspension and that 44% of first permanent exclusions and 42% of closest permanent exclusions were received over a year before the first serious violence offence.[19]

Almost six in ten children who had ever been permanently excluded had also been cautioned or sentenced for an offence, while,

---

17 Should prison education be different for women?, 2018, Prisoners' Education Trust.

18 Ministry of Justice cited in: Making the difference: breaking the link between school exclusion and social exclusion, 2017, Institute for Public Policy Research.

19 Education, children's social care and offending, 2022, Department for Education and Ministry of Justice.

shockingly, over one in five children who had ever been permanently excluded were also cautioned or sentenced for a serious violence offence. Of the children who had ever been persistently absent from school, 9% were cautioned or sentenced for an offence – highlighting the importance of keeping children in some form of education wherever possible.[20]

None of these statistics should be cause for apathy.

The data reinforces many of the anecdotal stories I have heard over many years about how a failure in SEN provision or undiagnosed SEN became an important factor that exposed a young person to exclusion and the criminal justice system.

Indeed, the Department for Education study[21] found that 80% of those who had been cautioned or sentenced for an offence and 87% of those cautioned or sentenced for a serious violence offence had been recorded as having SEN.

A further 95% of those whose offending had been prolific had been recorded as having SEN.

Overall, this survey and the continued research the Conservative Government is doing into this area is welcome, though it is not without its limitations. It doesn't count children involved in serious violence who have never had a caution or conviction, or every young person involved in criminal exploitation but not involved in serious violence.

What it does show though is that not being in school and lacking the protection of the education system can be a factor in putting a child at risk of involvement in serious violence.

We should always remember too that those who are seeking to exploit young people know this and do all they can to actively drive a wedge between them and their school, just as they do with

---

20   *Ibid.*
21   *Ibid.*

their families. Children being suspending and excluded from school is good news for those who recruit and exploit children for crime or sexual abuse. In fact, exploiters often positively encourage children to get into trouble at school – sometimes engineering exclusions by coercing children to carry drugs or weapons into school, knowing that being out of school makes them easier targets and more vulnerable.

Children are more likely to be exposed to child criminal exploitation outside of mainstream school, and being excluded can leave children feeling rejected and unwanted by the education system. Those with long experience of working with vulnerable children know that exploiters can prey on these feelings and build distrust on the reluctance of those children to seek support or protection from teachers, social workers, parents, or their family.

With a reported 'recruitment' target of 20% new young people at any time, the organised crime gangs can't afford to leave anything to chance. It's a vicious circle driven by a chilling and cruel aim to make children more isolated from the people who could protect them.

Sadly, it frequently works. Until professionals search out those children with the same level of determination to help them as the exploiters do to exploit them, it is going to continue. We need to up our game.

The impact of Covid on schools and their students, and its aftermath, has made everyone's task harder.

The Covid pandemic arrived almost a year before my term as Children's Commissioner for England came to end, so my last year in post was one that I couldn't ever have predicted. From the start, it was obvious that children were likely to get overlooked unless things changed. Rightly, the Government's emphasis was on protecting older and vulnerable people from the infection, but other countries seemed to be also thinking much more about the impact on children too. In some Scandinavian countries, the Prime Minister appeared on national TV within days with a special children's briefing – the sole aim to reassure children and to let them know that they are important and that those who are making decisions are thinking of them. No such broadcast ever happened in England, despite my direct requests to No. 10.

It was clear to me that children needed to be kept in the spotlight of decision-makers, and as Children's Commissioner, I focused heavily on the impact the virus and lockdowns were having on children's lives.

From the first week in lockdown, I was pushing the Government to keep schools open for the most vulnerable children, and throughout the pandemic, I continued to argue that the less time children spent out of school, the better.

During the summer of 2020, when it became clear that theme parks were going to reopen before children were allowed back in school, I was publicly critical of the Government's failure to put the interests of children first.

The UK Covid-19 Inquiry provides an opportunity to make sure lessons are learnt from the past and to put measures in place to ensure that children are never overlooked again during a national emergency.

Sadly, children being overlooked was a consistent theme throughout my time as Children's Commissioner. There were repeated failures by many in Whitehall to consider the impact of policies on children, and during the Covid pandemic, we saw the consequences.

Schools were closed for too long, and the disruption to children's education and the impact on their mental health this caused is now well established. Although schools were kept open for vulnerable children, few attended. What has become clear, too, is that a significant number of children have found it difficult to get back into the routine of going to school.

In the year following the lifting of the final school lockdown, I spoke to many teachers and school leaders about how Covid had changed school life for some vulnerable children, and almost every one of them could relay examples of children who had just stopped turning up to school after 2020. Children still tell me about the negative impact that Covid had on their experiences of school, including their ability to learn, their desire to be at school, the likelihood of returning to school, and a severe decline in their mental health because of the lockdowns. Many of these young people were experiencing mental health problems even before the pandemic.

Added to this, many parents struggled to teach their children from home, and for parents of children with SEND, this was particularly challenging. Many parents have told me how their once-confident children have been beset by anxiety and depression, unable to progress in school since the pandemic.

One girl, who set out on her GCSEs enjoying school and with high hopes from her teachers of doing well, emerged from the pandemic too anxious to go back into the classroom for more than an hour or two a week. Whilst the special educational needs co-ordinator (SENCO) had been supportive, this hadn't translated into support from education psychologists or from a mental health team. Now another year on, her mother had had to give up her job to help her daughter learn at home as best she could. They had given up on GCSEs and just wanted to get back to the normality of going to school.

This experience is echoed around the country, with tens of

thousands of children still really struggling with something that seemed such a normal part of life just a few years ago.

The increase in pupil absence was already a cause for concern before 2020. Persistent absence of more than 50% of school time more than doubled during the last decade, and the current estimates suggest as many as 100,000 school children in England are persistently absent from school.[22]

The statistics reinforce what I have heard from school leaders – that those most at risk of vulnerability prior to Covid were often the children hit hardest by the impact of the pandemic. There have been particularly large increases in persistent absence in special schools, and for those children with SEN support, the rate of absence is significantly higher than those children without SEN. The overall absence rate for pupils eligible for free school meals was 11.0% in autumn 2022. This compares to 6.3% for those pupils who were not eligible for free school meals.[23]

This severe absence has consequences for the children missing school. It disrupts their education and routine, and it removes what is a protective environment for many children. Over the last three years, I have heard many similar stories about the risks associated with absence from school, from children spending time wandering streets and parks during the day, open to exploitation and harm, to children suffering mental health problems.

It also impacts on a child's chances of achieving good qualifications when they leave full-time education. Children who miss school are also more likely to end up excluded from schools, and every extra day a child misses from school lowers their chances of achieving five or more good GCSEs and increases their chance of becoming 'not in education, employment, or training' (the Office

22 Thousands of children aren't turning up to school post-lockdown. Why?, 2022, Financial Times.
23 Pupil absence in schools in England, 2023, Department for Education.

for National Statistics publishes regular data setting out how many young people aged 16–24 are not in either education, employment, or on a training scheme).

Indeed, persistent absence from school is often an indicator of risk. It is revealing that just over half of young people who went on to receive a custodial sentence had been persistently absent from school.[24] Three years from the pandemic, there is great unease about the high numbers of children who are persistently absent from school – not attending 10% of the time. It has been estimated that over 100,000 children are severely absent – not attending 50% of the time.

These cases are often complex. Many children have suffered with poor mental health since lockdown and are too anxious to attend, some have additional needs or are awaiting assessment and support, some are living in chaotic households, and some have given up on school – fallen out of the habit altogether. It is a global problem, as I found out when I met a group of education leaders from around the world in 2023. But we need a solution – for the children who are missing an education and for our economy, which needs a skilled and talented workforce.

In July 2023, we were told that 30% of the children in Year 11, an exam year, were persistently absent and that 40% of disadvantaged children were persistently absent overall.[25] One secondary school told me that they had 500 children who were persistently or severely absent out of a school roll of 1,200. This isn't a blip – it's a disaster for those children and one that requires us all to look again at how we make school engaging and how we support the most vulnerable children to attend and do well.

---

24 The education and social care background of young people who interact with the criminal justice system: May 2022, Office for National Statistics.
25 Pupil absence in schools in England: autumn and spring terms, 2022, Department for Education.

There also are clear overlaps between children with additional unmet needs and non-attendance at school, which is why providing high-quality support to children with SEND should be the hallmark of an excellent education system. Of course, many children with SEND do receive a fantastic education, and there are many thousands of dedicated professionals working hard to give children with SEND the opportunities to learn and succeed that they have a right to expect. There are around 1.4 million children with a SEN in England, around 16% of all pupils, and the majority are educated in mainstream schools. This number has risen considerably over recent years. However, although the number of children with an EHCP grew by 10% in 2021, the number of pupils with SEN support increased by less than 0.5%.[26]

We know that children with SEN have markedly worse attainment than their peers without SEN. In 2019, only just over a quarter of children with SEN passed English and maths GCSEs, compared with 71% of children without SEN. Although four out of five children in AP have identified SEND, I have heard from many families that many are not receiving the support they need.[27]

Having SEN can have a huge impact on a child's life chances. The Government's 2022 Green Paper on SEN and AP[28] points out that at age 27, young people with SEN are 25% less likely to be in sustained employment than their peers with no identified SEN.

In 2019, I authored and presented a Dispatches documentary for Channel 4 looking at the rise of home education, called Skipping School: Britain's Invisible Kids. I met families with children with SEN who hadn't received the support they needed from their

---

26   Briefing: Five things you need to know about SEN in schools, 2021, Children's Commissioner.

27   *Ibid.*

28   SEND Review: Right support, right place, right time, 2022, Department for Education and Department of Health and Social Care.

school – or in some cases multiple schools – and as a result had ended up having to move schools repeatedly or eventually dropping into 'home education' because there seemed no other alternative.

What was so shocking was how school life crumbled over weeks and months to the point where some children were so desperately unhappy and unable to cope that they were threatening to kill themselves if they were made to go to school. Terrified of what might happen and desperate to keep their children safe, parents responded in the only way they felt they could by taking their child out of school to be educated at home until they could get a place in a school that could provide more support and care.

I met one family whose daughter had been to 15 different schools in less than ten years. This very bright and self-sufficient child, who had been diagnosed with autism, told me how she coped in difficult situations – taking time out of the classroom, having sensory objects around her, writing things down to express how she felt – all things she had found helped her, but they were often seen as disruptive by the school. Although it had been agreed that teachers should allow her to use her strategies to self-regulate, she was often told she couldn't leave the classroom, which left her more and more anxious and distressed.

She showed me a list she had made of what a good school for her would look like: being orderly and well run, clear timetables that didn't change so you always knew where you should be, good discipline and quiet corridors, polite and respectful conversations in the classroom, teachers who know you and are there to help you learn.

Isn't that what everyone would want from a good school, I asked? It was, but it took her another two years to find one that could give her and her parents the confidence that this time it was going to be OK. I heard from her and her mum after she received great GCSE results and as she was preparing to start sixth form.

According to the Department for Education, 116,000 children were home schooled over 2021/22, a number that has skyrocketed from 55,000 in 2018/19.

While there have always been parents who make a philosophical decision to teach their children at home, and that number is likely to have risen due to home schooling during the pandemic, most of those 116,000 children are not being taught at home because their parents have made a positive choice to home school. Many of them are there because they are being pushed into home education by a school system that isn't meeting their needs or able to cope with their behavioural issues.

I am in no doubt that some children with SEND are being deliberately managed out of mainstream education, either formally or informally, because schools have failed to understand or support their needs. Even Ofsted has raised the rising trend of exclusions among children and young people with SEND and how some children showing behaviours associated with ADHD and autistic spectrum disorder (ASD) who are undiagnosed are being excluded from mainstream schools because of their behaviour.

Some schools have been canny too about how they remove pupils they can't cope with and have used a variety of methods to remove children from the school roll. Ofsted's definition of off-rolling is taking a pupil off the school roll to try and manipulate exam results and league tables. A small number of schools have gamed league tables. It can be no coincidence that exclusions are high in Year 10.

Given that schools do not record the reason why a pupil has

been removed from a school roll unless in the case of a formal exclusion, it is impossible to be certain about the extent of off-rolling that is going on. When I ask headteachers whether off-rolling is still happening since I and others shone a spotlight on it, they say of course it is. Some schools have just got more sophisticated and are better at hiding it.

'Go and look at our school on an Ofsted assessment day and see if you can find the kids with SEND,' one parent said to me not long ago. 'You won't. They'll be at home because that's where the school suggested they stay over these disruptive few days.'

Of course, it doesn't happen everywhere, but parents have told me it happened to their child far too frequently for it to be a one-off.

A book, *Square Pegs*, written by Fran Morgan, who formed Square Peg in 2019 following her own daughter's struggles in the education system, and Ellie Costello, who joined her as Director in 2020, highlights the growing number of children with additional needs who are not thriving in a 'one-size-fits-all' education system. It describes the thousands of children who are trying to come to terms with a system that encourages conformity and who often suffer personally as a result. Full of practical advice and approaches, the book understands the pressures of narrow top-down systems with the realities of a growing number of children who are unable to fit in and cope. They are right to believe there is a different and better way.

We have allowed a culture and a system to grow that is sometimes excluding (formally and informally) some of the most vulnerable children. There may be thousands of children who are being excluded, off-rolled, or 'manage moved' off school rolls for unjust and unnecessary reasons, and as result they are out of school and at greater risk of not only leaving education without good qualifications but also falling into danger.

Some of these children will not even go through an official exclusion process, so they are not captured by statistics, even though to all intents and purposes they have been removed from a school roll. They could be in another mainstream school, AP, an independent school, a special school, or home education.

We have also developed a system where sending children to 'Alternative Provision', never to return, is tolerated. This can be provision that is often not meeting the needs of many of those children, some of them very vulnerable, who are outside mainstream schools. At the time of the 2019 school census, around 16,000 children in England were being educated in state-supported AP, with around 45% of those children having been permanently excluded from school. While some APs do remarkable things and are very good, others are frequently not providing the necessary opportunities that we give to children in mainstream schools.

The academic outcomes for many of the children who end up out of mainstream education and placed in AP are just not good enough. Only 1 in 20 children in AP passed English and maths at GCSE before the pandemic.[29] This is hardly surprising given attendance rates for children in AP are also poor and that fewer than half of the children who spend time in AP in Year 11 make a return to a mainstream school.

Children in AP are also some of our most vulnerable young people, including those at risk of criminal exploitation. They are more likely to have already had some interaction with the criminal justice system, more likely to have additional needs, and more likely to have SEND than children in mainstream schools. Sadly, some PRUs and AP settings are seen as little more than a dumping ground for 'difficult' children.

I do recognise that some AP provides a nurturing environment

---

29 Warming the cold spots of alternative provision: a manifesto for system improvement, 2020, The Centre for Social Justice.

with higher levels of pastoral care and support and a skilled staff team who are able to help young people learn and gain qualifications. My criticism of Alternative Providers is not a judgement on the professionals who work in them, more the lack of attention and effort that government has put into improving them.

The fact is the AP system is highly inconsistent, and it is not organised or funded adequately to support every child to succeed. In many AP settings, there is no real vision of excellence. This is not helped by the lack of in-depth analysis of what makes a good AP setting by the Department for Education. The deep relationships that need to be built to support vulnerable children through their school life are rarely built in AP, and there is often a consistent lack of care.

I don't think AP is yet structured to help most children back into mainstream school and to support them to stay there. Too often, it is a one-way street that takes children out of school but does not return them to the classroom as the intention should be. Often, children are put onto reduced timetables – sometimes of just a few hours a week – and taxied in and out of different settings, and at worst, they can spend hours being organised into lessons or waiting for their sessions with tutors.

Too often, AP seems to be housed in poor shabby buildings with loose timetables and poor attendance. Sometimes when I've visited an AP setting, I've seen children just wandering around or locked in a room – obviously, neither is inspiring or good for the child. Some feel like prisons; others are unstructured, under-staffed, and underqualified to deal with children there who are affected by trauma. Many have children with undiagnosed SEN being placed into an environment that can leave them vulnerable to grooming and exploitation.

Is it surprising that many children don't thrive in this kind of environment?

I have spoken to many people in the criminal justice system

who are concerned about the links between the criminal justice system and AP, in particular PRUs. I have heard PRUs described as 'job centres for criminals' – places where vulnerable young people are gathered in one place for those who wish to exploit them.

I can't help feeling that too many children in PRUs are being set up to fail and that too little attention is being given to the root causes of their problems at school, which often stem from what is happening at home or elsewhere. While learning in smaller classes in a PRU will benefit some children, aspirations for achievement are too low. Almost no child who attends a PRU will go on to university, other than perhaps much later in life.

We are also sometimes exposing vulnerable children with no involvement with criminal exploitation to children who have experience of or are involved in crime. It is an enormous risk. Victims of trauma are also being sent to the same establishment as perpetrators.

It makes no sense to place a 14-year-old teenage mum, with very specific needs, in the same 'Unit' as a child who has a conviction for knife crime, who has their own very different needs. All of this is as far away as is imaginable from a system that identifies vulnerable children with additional needs and provides the timely nurture and support they need to enable them to learn and succeed in school alongside their peers. The need for a more inclusive, trauma-informed, and trauma-responsive education system is more important than ever.

CHAPTER 5

Inclusion Not Exclusion

Ask most of us as adults about our childhood and we will talk about the schools we attended and the experiences we had there. A good school experience helps us achieve academically but it also helps us define our identity, shapes our values, provides a sense of belonging and community, and builds our skills and confidence to succeed throughout life. 'What school did you go to?' 'What year?' 'Do you remember that time?' These are the moments at school that bind us together.

But imagine you didn't go to school very much. 'Where did you grow up?', someone I took to a YOI said to a teenager who was busy making us coffee as part of his barista training. 'Ah, which school?' he said enthusiastically when learning they were from the same town. 'I didn't really go to school,' the boy said, and no one, including the boy himself, really knew what to say next.

This boy and the other children who fall out of the school system miss a lot, and the effect can be devastating. It can fuel a sense of alienation and so often it can be the tipping point into crisis and harm. We don't talk about it enough and we don't try hard enough to make sure it doesn't happen.

As I've said repeatedly, our youth justice system is full of young people who have been excluded or suspended, or have fallen out of the education system – many with no regular schooling since their primary years. It is difficult to believe how this can happen so often with such regular patterns and consequences. I have spoken to many children and professionals who have told me about how being excluded or moved out of school will often trigger a downward spiral and how children can become stuck in a twilight world of slow referral processes, occasional home tutoring, two-hours-a-week timetables, and isolation from friends. Without the routine, the relationships, the protective factors of school, they are out on a limb and often highly visible and vulnerable to those who wish to exploit them.

The challenge is to make these children highly visible to the education system again – children on whom the spotlight rests and is interested in rather than passing over them in search of the high achievers.

I am optimistic that it can be done and that we can improve the education experience of the group of young people who are at risk of missing out and improve their life chances – as we should.

How do we give all children the attention, support, and encouragement they need to be able to achieve great things in school?

The shelves are full of reports that tell us what it takes for these children to succeed, which is quickly reaffirmed by visits to and conversations with inspiring schools that are doing it. My optimism is founded on those school leaders, teachers, and organisations I've met over recent years who have built a positive and inclusive school environment that is there for everyone. They have a clear message: this school is here to support all children to succeed, including the most vulnerable.

We know, from the success stories we hear, that it is very possible, and it is time it was a priority for everyone in the education system – including those at the top of government.

A school or college rooted firmly in its local community, which has built up trust with families and children over many years and works hand in glove with other local services and organisations is a model for a more inclusive, nurturing, and ultimately success-ful education.

It's a good sign when you go into a school and the reception is busy. Every time I have been to Surrey Square Primary School in south London I've walked through the door to a buzz of conver-sation with parents and family members waiting to talk to staff. I know another school that calls its reception area the 'front room', as it's so well known as a community meeting space. It's not sur-prising when you see how much is going on to help families – food banks, washing machines for children to wash their uniforms, a room to have breakfast, or a breakfast session for all the children who want to come. One school told me they opened at 6.30am and had a hundred children in the building by 7am. The headteacher told me they know they need to open at that time, otherwise these children would be hanging around in the local park, and that's where trouble can start.

In his school, family support workers go along to the housing office with families, they advise on how to manage debt, they re-fer them to health support, and they work with them to support their children to learn. This isn't to distract from the learning, far from it. It is to help support a young person who may otherwise fail to learn.

The Oasis Southbank Academy in Waterloo is now able to say that it has more young people leaving the school to go to Oxbridge than it used to have leaving and going to prison (of which thank-fully there are no longer any).

How did they achieve this? By building a scaffolding of support throughout their children's school years, by spending hours and hours sitting with families and helping to support them through their problems, and then – the big one – having ambition for those children, an unswerving belief that each child could achieve great things. From early nurture and encouragement right through to help with university applications and even lifts to take the family to visit when their child has gone away to study, children are supported throughout. Many are now at top universities and the cycles of underachievement and vulnerability to crime are being broken.

Look what can be done, I tell people, and then ask yourself why we aren't doing the same everywhere.

We should celebrate the thousands of excellent schools throughout the country that are delivering such remarkable educational opportunities and support for some of the most vulnerable young people. I know that teaching and school staff care deeply about the children they teach and that the support and inspiration that many vulnerable children receive from their school enables them to go on and progress well in life – for some, preventing potential problems occurring and escalating. In any gathering of schools throughout the country, there are inspirational stories of schools that are supporting families, employing mentors, youth workers, and social workers, and working with communities to give their students the best chance possible. Yet we notice them by their extraordinary work. Being inclusive is not yet mainstream enough.

So, we must also be true to those young people who have not had a positive experience of school and are unlikely to progress into adulthood with the qualifications and skills that they need to be able to fulfil their potential. Too often, these children have been viewed as a problem that can be pushed onto someone else to deal with. It is their success in education that we need to focus on far more than we do currently.

I have seen many programmes and interventions that have been established to enable some vulnerable children to have a more positive learning experience. At the heart of their success is always a drive to be inclusive and to recognise that all children will develop and learn in different ways and that some will need extra support.

A starting point must be to have an education system that appeals to those children for whom school is currently neither enjoyable nor fulfilling and often inadequate in preparing them for the next stages of their lives. We have seen too many shifts in the school curriculum that have squeezed out a lot of the creativity that fires up our curiosity and love of learning. We have created an environment for some children that makes them more likely to switch off. These are the children who feel school is 'not for them'.

I believe there are two broad and fundamental aspects of the system that need to change.

First, it is very clear to anyone who cares to take a look that the 'failure rate' of the current education system is far too high and that the way the system drives some schools' priorities is very apparent to many of the children who are most likely to struggle. Some of the most distressing conversations I have had with children are when they describe their experiences of education and schools as being unwelcoming or 'not there for them'.

The phenomenon of the 'forgotten third' of children who leave school at 19 without a basic level of qualification is happening for a reason, and it is difficult to believe, but we have become almost complacent about it. In the world of industry, which manufacturing process would tolerate a failure rate of a third? A third of the products made are broken or not fit for sale. Not quite the analogy for children but you can see my point. The answer is none – it wouldn't be accepted. Then why do we think it's acceptable for children's education? There seems to be very little debate about why it is happening and the scandalous loss of opportunity for both young people and the country as a whole.

The second aspect is the limitations of the curriculum and its focus on learning for exams. Children often say that the curriculum does not interest them, which leads to a waning interest in learning or sometimes even to be at school. Back in 2018, the House of Commons Education Select Committee took evidence when looking into the high rate of school exclusions, and it concluded that the narrow nature of the curriculum could be one contributing factor. The RSA (Royal Society for the encouragement of Arts) also published a study showing that some young people become more engaged with school when changes to the curriculum are made, particularly where there is greater opportunity to participate in art.

This lack of creativity in the curriculum is the foundation of so much of the disaffection with schools that I hear from many young people. We have a generation of children able to find out about anything they want at the push of a button – and they do. On any day, they are creating film, written content, spoken word, art, games, and experiences, and communicating on a mass scale. They drink in content and culture from all over the world through interactions on social media. Their horizons are vast, their mindsets open, and their ability to learn – especially on a digital platform –nothing short of astonishing. Yet all that can shrink once they step inside school.

It feels like we are running an education system on analogue, years after the world switched over to digital.

There is also a particular deficit in the current curriculum for Minoritised Ethnic young people, who often say that the school's curriculum as it is currently made up feels outdated and partial. Of course, some of this is about our interpretation of the past and the history of black communities in Britain. But it is not solely confined to history. The English literature curriculum has been seriously lacking in ethnic diversity, and the main characters in children's books are almost eight times more likely to be animals than people of colour.[1] A 2020 study by Teach First found that the biggest exam board, accounting for almost 80% of GCSE English literature entries, did not feature a single book by a black author, and featured only two books by Minoritised Ethnic authors.[2]

Being able to see and hear yourself in what you are learning can be the difference between wanting to be in school and not, and in stopping young people from falling out of education. Feeling like you 'belong' in your classroom is so important.

A report by Penguin in 2020[3] summed up what so many children are missing out on, saying 'Literature is a curator of our imaginations, and schools are the caretakers of the education of young people – who are being denied access to the glorious, outstanding, and often groundbreaking narratives coming out of Britain's Black and Asian communities.'

There is already evidence that a more diverse and representative curriculum can have a direct positive impact on students' attendance and achievement, so why is it not being implemented across the education system?

Educational initiatives by groups such as The Black Curriculum are helping us move towards black history forming a key part of the curriculum, but government itself needs to be more engaged in providing arts-focused black history programmes and teacher training that focuses on influential black historical and contemporary people. A 2023 survey of 35,000 school children found that

---

1   Children's books eight times as likely to feature animal main characters as BAME people, 2020, The Guardian.
2   Missing pages: campaign for greater diversity in the GCSE English literature syllabus, 2020, Teach First.
3   Lit In colour: diversity in literature in English schools, 2021, The Runnymede Trust and Penguin Books.

three quarters said that they wanted to learn more about the Windrush generation in school.[4]

Adapting the curriculum to engage children who currently feel it is 'not for them' will be a vital component in narrowing the attainment gap between disadvantaged Minoritised Ethnic children and their peers. It should be a part of making schools more inclusive, somewhere that all children are excited about attending. But it won't happen of its own accord; government will need to lead that drive.

There is so much that a national campaign led by the Department for Education, and schools themselves, could achieve to increase the numbers of school governors, school board members, and those in a position of school leadership from Minoritised Ethnic backgrounds, as well as greater transparency about the ethnic diversity of those involved in senior decision-making in a school. Over recent years, governing school and college boards have been told to collate and publish their own diversity data – which is a welcome step – but it will take much more to encourage and support a change at the top to really represent our diverse communities.

We also need to increase the number of black teachers in our classrooms, particularly in leadership roles. Race-equality training should be in all teacher training and embedded as a core module at the new national flagship Institute of Teaching. There also needs to be an awareness that the SEN of black and mixed heritage boys can often be overlooked by schools.

These reforms are badly needed but on their own will only go so far.

---

4   Should we learn about the Windrush Generation at school?, 2023, Votes for Schools.

We need to look to those who are already delivering a very different experience for young people, with very different outcomes for those most at risk of harm or low attainment. Those school leaders tell me how their pursuit of support to help all children succeed has not only improved educational achievement but also reduced exclusions to single figures.

One woman who knows about changing the culture of the education system is Maureen McKenna who was Director of Education at Glasgow City Council for 14 years. When Maureen took up her post, exclusions in Glasgow were at an all-time high. One secondary school had 770 exclusions in one year; some had a revolving door, where children would arrive at school, and then an incident would happen, and they would be sent straight out of the door again. Maureen felt this was an approach that was doing nothing to improve outcomes or life chances for a significant number of teenage children and set about changing it.

She set out with a simple but important mission: to break the habit of exclusions. Before she agreed to sign an exclusion, she asked for two sets of information – three reasons why the child should be excluded and three things the school had done to prevent it happening. Such was the power of the new form that things started to change fast, with a new focus on keeping children in school.

This determination to reduce exclusions ran alongside the work of the VRU in Glasgow. Its focus on tackling crime as a public health issue and tackling its root causes has been pioneering, and its ethos and is now being followed by VRUs across the country. In Glasgow there has been an 88% reduction in school exclusions over the last decade, while youth crime dropped 50% over the same period.[5]

Glasgow City Council changed its local guidance to schools so that exclusion was no longer seen as a 'final sanction', which it argued was incompatible with promoting inclusion, learning, development, and wellbeing. While there is no 'zero exclusions' policy in the city, its guidance states that children have an inalienable right to an education and that it is the duty of the local authority, each school, and every member of staff to create the relationships and environment within which prevention and early intervention can support every child.

These principles of a whole-school ethos of prevention, early intervention, and support are key to the promotion of positive relationships, learning, and behaviour. Glasgow's guidance says exclusion should be as short as possible, always have a positive and purposeful intention for the learning and wellbeing of a child, and should not be viewed as punitive. It should be a proportionate response where there is no appropriate alternative, and the time during and after the exclusion period should be used constructively to ensure positive support is in place.

Maureen's ambition was to create a system that nurtures children – a far cry from what she saw as a 'deficit' system focused on failure rather than strengths. There wasn't a culture of inclusion, and every part of the system was sending out a message that children needed to be fixed – they are the ones that need to conform – not the system. Often children were having to go out of school and do intensive work elsewhere and then be brought back to school. There was a range of provision outside the city, so children were being transported outside the boundaries. It was expensive and

---

5   Glasgow education chief: schools were excluding pupils out of habit, 2021, BBC News.

time-consuming and was not child-centred, and there was a lack of compassion and care for families. It was all about staff, and structures and processes – not children.

Maureen and her team began by defining the principle and meaning of nurture explicitly, including forming a nurture steering group led by a psychologist. It was science led. For Maureen, nurturing is about how we talk, the language used, and how we relate to families. The focus in schools changed to provide support to children in school, with specialists working alongside teachers rather than spending money on taxis to ferry children miles away. This in turn grew the capacity and knowledge of teachers. Maureen's ethos was that while some children do need specialist provision, every child has a right to learn alongside their peers.

She argues that if you can give a high-quality offer to children, they will respond positively, but when sparks fly it is often because children are having to conform to the way teachers teach. She believes that because children are all different, teachers need to change their approach and reflect on how they approach learning. That should mean investing in the craft of teaching and empowering headteachers.

Maureen also believes that it isn't just about more money – it's about what you do with what you have and repurposing when necessary. That means, in her words, stop doing the 'fluff' in schools. In other words, if something doesn't impact on what happens in the classroom, then don't do it. It also means implementing a curriculum that meets children's needs, that sparks their interest, and that makes them want to come into school. That could be politics, psychology, photography. When children don't feel like they are learning in school, they are less likely to want to go to school, because school doesn't feel like it is working for them.

Maureen's push back against an established status quo had tangible results, and her leadership and vision should be a template for others to replicate. In 2023, Maureen was recruited by the London VRU to bring down exclusions in London. A positive move in my view.

The question is: why aren't more areas following the same path?

I've concluded that for many areas, there hasn't been the encouragement or incentives to do so. Certainly, the behaviour policies that schools are expected to follow hardly encourages it. Neither is inclusion measured by Ofsted. Too often, it is viewed as a distraction from achieving academic results.

With so few incentives to be inclusive and so many that work against it, we have been stuck on a hopeless see-saw weighted against those children who need extra help to be able to succeed. I think things are changing, but there is certainly a long way to go until all children get the education we would all want them to have.

There is so much evidence about children with SEND, autism, learning disabilities, and additional needs struggling in the classroom and too many falling out of school as a result. Additional needs go unidentified or misdiagnosed, and labelled as 'misbehaviour', which leads to suspension or permanent exclusion.

The policy for children with SEND in school was set by the Children and Families Act 2014, which is one of those pieces of legislation with very good intentions but lacking the follow-through to make these aims a reality. The Act requires education, health, and social care agencies to work together more closely than they have in the past.

However, the focus it has put on EHCPs as the main way of helping children has driven support towards those who have a higher level of needs. This has meant that children with lower levels of SEND often receive little support, leaving problems to develop and escalate. It has also driven a high-cost system, access to which is often contested through litigation and appeals.

I have met many parents who tell me how their children didn't apply for a plan because the whole process was so onerous, they couldn't face it. One parent, a senior manager in her day job, who had successfully secured a plan for her child, told me it was like trying to get a PhD.

Even she nearly gave up, so imagine what it must be like for parents who aren't used to dealing with this sort of thing.

What is often so striking about the conversations I have with parents whose children with SEN are not receiving support is the lack of apparent purpose and clarity in the response to the way their young children were behaving in school. Rather than seeing their behaviour as warning signs that triggered specialist support in school, they had been dealt with through an endless carousel of referrals and assessments – sometimes taking many months and even years, disrupting their education along the way. We focus on the child as a problem – we don't look at how we can change the system.

> Amongst the group of mums that I met in north London, whose children had all been excluded repeatedly from school, six of the seven children who had experienced either a fixed-term or permanent exclusion had been diagnosed with SEN. Some of the children had been sent to AP, and one child to a PRU, where they were the youngest children in the school. They sat by themselves in an empty room as all the other children were so much older. What a depressing thought: a five-year-old, who should be excited to go into school, see friends, and have fun learning, sitting without any children of his own age.

Unsurprisingly, the parents I met were horrified and did not think that this kind of environment was going to help their child or keep them safe, even more so when they visited and also found there were police and high security on site.

So many families have told me that they give up on applying for help – or so often get their applications rejected – that you have to wonder if the middle classes are the only ones who can get through the EHCP hoops without help.

You would hope not, but there are plenty of signs that many children are not getting the help they need because they don't have a plan to guarantee help. With such a complex process, it is easy to see why some parents do just give up.

At one AP school I visited in east London where children had been excluded, an independent assessor judged that 85% of the children attending should be eligible for an EHCP. Unfortunately, just 15% had a plan. The others were left to struggle without help and in some cases become more vulnerable to violence and crime.

If the EHCP is going to be more than a middle-class offer, it needs to become more accessible, and support needs to be available for children much earlier to prevent crisis.

In fact, there is almost a dreadful inevitability in many of the stories I hear from those parents whose children with SEN have fallen out of the school system.

It is not surprising that some parents feel they have no other option than to take their children out of school to educate them at home after months or years of problems.

While off-rolling is not quite as blatant as it once was, discussions about a child's future that lead up to a decision to remove them from the school roll can happen over many weeks and the process can be a subtle one.

No school will say that they off-roll children, but some parents I have met have a very different opinion.

Some feel that some schools can hold negative opinions of

those parents who are making 'unrealistic demands' about receiving support for their children, rather than accepting that children with SEN or suffering from adverse childhood experiences have needs that should be expected and not seen as 'abnormal'. In some cases, the school describes their children as very smart, completing work quickly but then becoming bored and distracted, which the school views as misbehaviour. Some families have even told me how they were referred to social care as part of the process – something that most felt had been inappropriate and unhelpful.

There are fantastic schools who are showing there is a better way.

I first visited Vic Goddard, the headteacher of Passmore Academy in Essex best known for appearing in the Channel 4 series 'Educating Essex', when I was making the 'Dispatches' documentary for Channel 4 about children out of school. The school is big, busy, and full of life, with lots of personal interaction and plenty of stuff going on. It's also a school that is clearly all about its pupils – and that means all of them. Vic and the team have done all they can to build inclusivity and responsiveness into the school, accepting that for some young people, the normal school rules can't apply. Here, school rules aren't 'one size fits all' and their aim is to develop better-rounded human beings as a result.

Passmore has an access centre that opens at 6.30am and closes at 6pm, with adult supervision. It is a safe space for vulnerable children who don't enjoy the hullaballoo of school, somewhere they can feel comfortable. There are breakout rooms for time out, sensory rooms, skilled and trained staff, and a positive approach to championing children with special needs within the school.

Putting children with SEN first is at the heart of the Passmore ethos. Walk around Vic's school with him and you can't fail to be impressed by what you see: pride in the inclusive approach that values all children, breakout and calming rooms to help vulnerable children with their coping strategies and provide specialist support for children who need it, assemblies where it is the children with SEN who are taking the lead and presenting. You are left in no doubt that this school is for all children in the community, and parents are beating down the door to get a place as a result.

With the will to make these changes, providing this kind of support in schools should be so straightforward.

The Autism in Schools project works with autistic children and their families to develop practical ways schools can improve the experience for children who are finding school a challenge. They are working with mainstream and special schools in a person-centred approach so that teaching staff understand the challenges faced by individual students and can put necessary adjustments in place. This can help autistic children and their families to better understand their own challenges and strengths, increase self-confidence and self-awareness, reduce isolation, and improve relationships between families and schools. Parents have spoken about how transformative it has been. Teachers too can see the difference it makes – the 'best thing' they've ever been involved with according to one experienced teacher I met.

Of course, schools need to be able to respond to children who are disrupting a classroom and even on some occasions putting other children and/or staff at risk. All parents would expect this to be the case. But excluding a child from school when they are not even out of primary school is short-sighted and sometimes harmful. Being taken out of the environment where their friends are learning and growing up together can have a huge impact on children.

The children I met in north London who had been excluded from school in their first years of primary school were now being supported through one-to-one support in a mentoring scheme and were flourishing. They were setting their sights high and told me about their dreams of becoming doctors, teachers, social workers, and an engineer. These children very obviously have real talent and a bright future ahead of them, but the schools they were excluded from didn't seem able to see it or to properly harness it. With access to better support and a more inclusive, nurturing approach across the school, they should have been able to.

We also need a fundamental reset of AP. The Government's 2022 Green Paper on SEN and AP proposed making AP an integral part of local education systems and pledged to give AP schools funding stability to deliver a service focused on early intervention, as well as providing greater oversight and transparency around pupil movements. It called for a new national framework for AP to be delivered by an integrated SEND and AP system with national standards.

There are some brilliant AP providers and organisations who are already providing high-quality provision. These are now getting more and more credit, and I hope that their experience and expertise will be channelled by government and school trusts everywhere.

The move by some schools to set up their own internal 'Alternative Provision' or specialist support is very welcome. The charity The Difference has set up internal AP in one mainstream school called 'The Base'. This is somewhere school staff and children can take time to understand children's needs, build relationships, and work together to build support. Having this integrated internal resource gives students the chance to share their experiences of home and family, school, and community life, and bring agencies together to share information as well.

The combination of closer attention being paid to vulnerable children, conversations with trusted adults, and more inclusive practices allows the school to operate in a less siloed way, integrating the specialist 'alternative' provision into the rest of the school. The Difference makes an important assumption – one that we should all heed – that most children at some point in their lives are likely to need help – with their learning or wellbeing, or because they feel unsafe in some way. Once we make this assumption, we can respond with much better support, and sooner.

In Leeds, the Carr Manor Community School, part of the Leeds Learning Alliance group of 12 schools, has its own specialist provision in CATCH Leeds with which it works in partnership as part of its family of schools. CATCH Leeds is a community organisation that runs programmes and activities for young people, with a farm and horticulture on site. Children take part in restorative programmes with a strong emphasis on volunteering and participation. Schools reserve and pay for places each year to provide 'in-house' AP for children for a period of time before returning to the mainstream school. Children never leave the school roll. They are nurtured and encouraged in a supportive environment with a strong emphasis on responsibilities. None of its students have been excluded from the family of schools in 13 years.

Another approach is also being trialled in Croydon by the charity Oasis with an emphasis on youth support, mentors, and navigators in and around schools.

The year 2021 was the worst year to date for teenage murders in London. There were 30 in total, and five of them happened in Croydon – more than any other borough in the capital. The fifth was the fatal stabbing of a 15-year-old student, an Oasis student, on 30 December 2021. Oasis runs over 50 schools in some of the most deprived parts of the country and has since committed to overturning Croydon's reputation as 'London's knife crime capital'.

Oasis is creating a new model that it believes can be applied across the UK, in a new Croydon-wide collaborative, integrated education and youth service to support children to succeed in education and life. Its ambition is to create a revolutionary preventative approach to stem Croydon's epidemic of youth violence by working to keep young people in – and engaged with – mainstream education and the local community.

Oasis hopes to roll out this model in other parts of the country over the next few years, providing mentoring support to students (and staff) to keep children on roll and flourishing. It will support students through short-term and temporary intensive placements that offer them therapeutic time out of their mainstream school so they can return to it as soon as possible. It will also be providing a smaller number of long-term places in order to support those students who are unable to continue their education in a mainstream school but, again, with the long-term goal of return, if possible.

The belief that this is essential to the battle to end youth violence – ongoing, one-to-one personal support and mentoring for every young person struggling and at risk of school exclusion – is so important and one I wholeheartedly agree with. The programme coordinates and partners with the large range of small and local 'grassroots' youth work, youth mentoring, and parent support organisations that have grown up in Croydon. These are innovative examples of how we can move the system away from disparate AP and focus on internal specialist support to enable children to stay in school.

The Conservative Government is beginning to look at this new 'internal' approach to AP but in my view, we need to see projects and services like them everywhere to deliver a complete overhaul of the way we label 'Alternative Provision' to become specialist support, something more inclusive, long-lasting, and appealing to both children and parents.

I want to see a system where this kind of inclusion and bespoke support runs through the culture of our schools like a stick of rock.

It is the only way forward, but it will take leadership and new expectations, funding – investing in support that children need, and accountability to deliver.

CHAPTER 6

Partnerships Around School to Support Young People to Succeed

Despite the mountain of difficulties so many children with SEND or other vulnerabilities deal with, I do believe most schools want to be supportive, and I'm encouraged that many schools are already making inclusiveness a top priority. Exclusion rates are too high, and we should be concerned about those, but it is encouraging that almost 90% of the exclusions that do happen take place in only 10% of schools. Most schools are doing reasonably OK.[1]

While these statistics don't include some of the tricksy techniques some schools use to remove 'disruptive' children from their classrooms, they do at least suggest that most schools are doing well to keep children in their school.

But this does mean that it's not only the characteristics and actions of the child that leads to them being excluded; it's also about the culture of the school.

For those schools that do exclude, the question is whether they have lower levels of support for children with SEN, and stricter

---

1   Excluded teens are often the most vulnerable – and they're falling through the gap, 2019, Children's Commissioner.

behaviour policies that make them more intolerant. Unfortunately, there is no data available to tell us, but it is probably both. Some may also just be more poorly managed.

What is clear is that if a school chooses to find alternatives to excluding children, there are plenty of models and interventions that can show it how.

Over the last few years, I have visited and spoken with many organisations that are making interventions every day to stop children from falling out of school and into harm. I've already described some of them. Many are run by small charities and voluntary groups, or individuals who have felt the effect of violence themselves. They work tirelessly to help children have a better future – sometimes with little recognition and uncertain funding. Our communities are richer for them, and some young people undoubtedly owe their success and in some cases their life to their dedication and support.

Every child who is suspended, off-rolled, or excluded makes their job harder. For those children who are not getting the support they need, their job is even more vital. However, the stories of schools that choose to operate a nurturing and inclusive culture are becoming more and more frequently heard.

We need culture change in all our schools, alongside financial support, that replicates the amazing work that is being done by some schools and by those small organisations and charities that are helping children to succeed in a system that has so often incentivised schools to exclude them.

Mentors in Violence Prevention is Scotland's largest anti-violence schools programme, which operates in 25 local authority areas and works to empower students to speak out safely against all forms of violence from knife crime to domestic violence or sexual harassment, and has been doing excellent work since it was adopted by the SVRU in 2011. Working in partnership with

Education Scotland, it is now operating in 130 secondary schools. The programme trains senior pupils to act as peer mentors who then deliver sessions to younger students in the school.

There are encouraging signs that other areas are working more strategically too. Some VRUs and Police and Crime Commissioners are using their coordinating and brokering role to bring partners together. In London, the VRU has put a focus on reducing school exclusions and has invested in nurtureuk and Tender – charities that support inclusion in schools – working in primary and secondary schools across London in areas of high violence. The programmes support children with SEN, support speech and language, help to build relationships, and tackle exclusions.

In Manchester, where the partnerships with local authorities – here, the Greater Manchester Combined Authority – are probably the most advanced of anywhere in the country, the VRU is supporting School Engagement Officers to provide training and safety advice, make better use of diversion schemes to lead young people away from criminality and onto positive pathways to help prevent them from entering the criminal justice system, and develop activities that help build positive relationships between police and young people. It is also supporting the excellent Football Without Borders scheme in schools, which uses football coaching and teamwork to build the engagement and confidence of children who are struggling and so build positive behaviour and engagement with school, as well as mentoring and group work. It's scheme that I've seen light up interest in school for children, with dramatic changes in commitment and purpose.

In the West Midlands, the VRU is working with data, evidence, and community groups to tackle the roots of exploitation and violence. It is supporting training to help teachers better identify and help keep safe pupils who are caught up in gangs and violence, including understanding the risks faced by vulnerable girls. It is also supporting online safety workshops that enable primary and secondary schools, teachers, and parents to work together to keep young people safe online.

In Thames Valley, the VRU is knitting together local community sector partners around schools. With lots of agencies in a room, they discuss cases and problems that are emerging contextually, with partners able to offer support and help with wider offers of support. It helps agencies understand the impact of childhood adversities and support a trauma-informed approach, also helping schools understand the wider support available and how they can help children stay in school and access help rather than excluding them. They are spearheading approaches to gather and use data to be able to identify where and when interventions are needed.

With many of these units now well established and increasingly embedded with their areas and local partner organisations, there is a real opportunity to make an impact. There would be even more so if they were working within a wider programme of reform to focus on early intervention and prevention and had some serious investment behind them.

Government-funded SAFE (Support, Attend, Fulfil, Exceed) pilot taskforces that run in ten hotspot areas of high violence over three years began in late 2022 to help schools and their partners support attendance, reduce exclusions, and focus on learning. The programmes are being evaluated but initial signs are promising.

The body of evidence of the benefits of school inclusion to support our young people to succeed and the model of intervention is growing exponentially.

In 2022, research by Royal Holloway University of London on children and young people permanently excluded from school in Surrey proposed how systems and services might work together to support school inclusion.[2] The research shows how the promotion of inclusive cultures and targeting interventions towards children and young people most at risk of exclusion can decrease the likelihood of escalation of behaviours that lead to exclusion.

The report praises the 'Short Stay Schools approach'[3] as providing excellent support for pupils with social, emotional, or mental health needs, and children with SEN. It also found a number of other solutions-based approaches, including the importance of early years and primary-to-secondary school transitions as being key developmental milestones/periods for intervention, a greater variety and availability of alternative options to exclusion such as pupil-centred, personalised interventions, short-term breaks at an alternative learning provision, and improved support for school staff in understanding the underlying causes of behaviour that might support a child-centred approach to supporting inclusion and reducing exclusion.

It is clear to me that the best route to help young people succeed is when the whole school and whole community work together.

When schools work with vulnerable children to show them the value of school, show them what success can look like, and help show parents what the opportunities for their children can look like, everything can change. It is about choosing to make school a positive place to be for all children, rather than a controlled punitive environment that many don't enjoy. All children have a right to an education – we need to ensure they get it.

I have been impressed with schools that wrap support services

---

2   Permanent school exclusions in Surrey: What works to keep children and young people in education?, 2022, Royal Holloway University of London.

3   Short Stay Schools are PRUs for children who have experienced difficultly in maintaining a place in mainstream education. They provide a range of programmes tailored to meet the needs of each individual student and assist children to reintegrate back into a suitable education setting.

around the school and identify children at risk of exclusion early on, create an education intervention plan, set out what the child's needs are and what has gone wrong, and co-construct what that plan is so that the child, parent, and school can work out what is going to happen next. Schools that are already doing this have barely had a permanent exclusion for years.

Vic Goddard told me that his school would receive a higher Ofsted grade if it took a more rigid approach to behaviour and curriculum but said he couldn't look at himself in the mirror if he did this. He sees the school as a community resource with an obligation to the whole community and the families who live in it – all of them. Vic also makes sure that any young person who doesn't get a family start to the day receives one at school. The school has food and toasters, microwaves, a fridge freezer, and washing machines – staff teach children how to wash their own clothes. The idea is to make children feel this is all part of the life of the school – they are not being labelled as different or vulnerable.

Oasis Community Learning take a similar approach in its 52 schools and has also been moving towards a trauma-informed practice approach, recognising that the level of adversity its students and their families experience is often impeding their learning and requiring a great deal of energy on the part of the families to manage.

It is piloting a programme of support in one of its primary schools to help 600 children and families, with a wraparound service of therapy, social work, provision of practical resources, advice, and joyful experiences. Now a year on, the work is becoming part of the way the school operates, with in-depth work with teachers and families. The pilot is called 'Oasis Nurture' because at the heart of it, the intention is to strengthen family resilience. The school got the highest results of all the Trust's primary schools this year – something I am sure is related.

This trauma-informed approach runs throughout Oasis secondary schools, where family workers, youth workers, and specialist teams provide intensive support for children and their parents through a community hub wrapped around the school. One youth worker told me that 65 children had been referred to their team for support over the last year – through building relationships and working with the young people to understand and help deal with problems, they had kept 63 of them in school – with two moving to a different area altogether.

One student, then in his final year at sixth form, summed up what it had meant for him:

> I've had my fair share of ups and downs and at times I felt unable to share my troubles and feelings with school and staff. I was fortunate to have a sanctuary which was the Hub Youth Team. The Youth Team were able to help me manage my emotions inside and outside of school. Without this support I wouldn't be the flourishing person I am today.

Part of that intensive support for children who are struggling will sometimes mean specialist support such as with communication, speech, and language problems. I was shocked when I discovered that more than 60% of young people in the youth justice system have difficulties with their speech, language, and communication.[4] Of children who persistently experience poverty, 75% arrive at school below average in language development, and around half of children in some areas of deprivation begin school with delayed language.[5] For some young people, language impairment is

---

4 Where SLTs work – justice settings, 2023, Royal College of Speech and Language Therapists.

5 Who needs oracy education most?, 2023, Oracy APPG.

associated with behaviour problems and, in turn, exclusion from mainstream schooling.

The work being done by the oracy education charity Voice 21 in PRUs in the last few years shows the positive impact that working on language impairment can have on young people's ability to self-regulate when confronted with something that triggers them. Most of the children it works with in PRUs have social, emotional, or mental health difficulties and find it very difficult to self-regulate. Teachers having a better understanding of oracy can help them to help children develop better self-regulation skills. It can boost children's confidence, particularly children with autism. This can also lead to a marked improvement in their behaviour at home, and there is evidence that high-quality oracy education can help to identify and respond to young people who are at risk of abuse or harm.

I don't think the education system appreciates often enough how the underlying causes of 'bad behaviour' that can lead to exclusion are very often related to adverse childhood experiences. When a deep dive into the root causes of serious violence in West Yorkshire was carried out, it showed how meaningful and rewarding education can be a protective factor against violence, exploitation, and other negative health outcomes.[6] Meanwhile, poor educational outcomes were being disproportionately suffered by children already experiencing inequality, something that is also replicated in the criminal justice system. Some of the children taking part in the research said that feeling inadequate at school was the start of a process that led to them feeling desperate for validation and much more vulnerable to those that were targeting and grooming children.

---

6   West Yorkshire response strategy refresh 2022: serious violence: West Yorkshire strategy for change, 2022, West Yorkshire Violence Reduction Unit.

It is hardly surprising to learn that programmes that increase educational inclusion and support children to succeed in school in deprived areas can also reduce violence and exploitation. School attainment, attendance, and good outcomes are protective factors against becoming involved in the criminal justice system.

It's also not surprising that whilst schools and others can help children by understanding and responding to the trauma of children's past, many of these traumas have their roots in early childhood and it is there that intervention is also needed at the earliest possible time to prevent problems escalating.

I have been banging the drum for providing support for children from their early years for decades. Children and their families do not fall into crisis overnight, and those children who struggle and fall behind before they start school are more likely to stay stuck behind their peers throughout childhood and into adulthood. The importance of establishing early attachments and healthy relationships as well as addressing parent stress, poor mental health, violent behaviour, and problematic substance use can't be overstated.

The educational impact of difficulties and trauma in early life are also significant. Children who are speaking and communicating well, who are curious and exploring the world, and who are making sense of numbers before school do better later in life. We also know that the educational attainment gaps between richer and poorer teenagers are already present at a very young age, with low-income children on average over a year behind their peers at school entry. Children with poor vocabulary skills are twice as likely to be unemployed when they grow up.

We know too how children who at an early age can manage their own emotions and behaviour go on to have much better outcomes later in life.

Babies and very young children can't regulate their emotions alone and need help from parents and carers, which in turn helps them learn to regulate their emotions independently. Children who are less able to control their feelings and behaviour in the early years are more likely to have worse long-term outcomes. They are more likely to struggle in education and in managing relationships with their peers.

The development check carried out by a nursery nurse or health worker when a child is 2–2.5 years old is an opportunity to identify additional need and respond with help, but the information is often not systematically collected or strategically considered and responded to. Whilst some children may get help after checks, many will not, and some miss out on the assessment altogether.

Children who fail to reach their development goals at five are more likely to have a social worker, more likely to be excluded from school and more likely to struggle with reading and writing at 11. By the age of five, 40% of the education disadvantage gap seen at age 16 is already in place.[7]

These gloomy predictions of future success are easily visible and clearly measured, yet they remain unseen and unacted on for many, leaving some children with a foundation of problems that will play out over years to come. As is so often the case, disadvantaged children and children with SEN are most likely to experience these setbacks in the early years of life.

Support in the early years can be transformational, helping families find solutions to the difficulties they are experiencing and providing children with the springboard they need to start school and the life ahead of them with a bounce.

The Conservative Government's Start for Life programme is set

---

7   Closing the disadvantage gap: a focus on the first five years, n.d., Education Policy Institute.

up to help provide the building blocks for lifelong emotional and physical health in the period from conception to the age of two. It is a supportive policy framework that is trying to improve children's lives, as well as saving billions from the expensive cost of social crisis, through improving school readiness and preventing later problems from bullying to poor mental health to addictions, criminality, and poor health. Its founder, Dame Andrea Leadsom MP, argues that securely attached infants are much more likely to go on to become adults who cope well with life's ups and downs and build strong relationships at work and at home, and are better equipped to raise their own children. I agree and I would like to see it expanded nationally.

The Early Intervention Foundation also agrees that access to early childhood education and care before the start of official schooling can maximise the life chances of children, particularly those from disadvantaged backgrounds. It can equip children with essential skills, including cognitive, self-regulatory, and social and emotional skills, which improves school readiness and outcomes in later life.

However, even more crucial than the provision of these services is the quality of the care provided. High-quality formal provision does improve outcomes for children, and improving school readiness and closing the disadvantage gap will not be achieved through early education and care alone. Other factors, like maternal education, family size, parent-child relationships, and the home environment, can have a larger impact than early education and care.

That is why activities and services like parenting programmes can be so important. Identifying the moments in a vulnerable child's life when they need extra support and intervention is something that various school, health, and social care systems have not always done consistently. The proof is in those Serious Case

Reviews. Too often, the intervention comes far too late, by which time crisis is already occurring or plans are not put in place to manage big changes in children's lives.

I've heard many distressing stories about vulnerable children falling into danger around the time they transition from primary to secondary school. Parents of children who end up involved in the criminal justice system, serious violence, or exploitation often say how the move from primary to secondary school was the period when problems really escalated.

Moving from the small, intimate primary school, where there are strong links to families and the community, to a larger secondary and sudden independence can be overwhelming for some. The size and scale of a new school can increase the pressure as children struggle to find their own identity, develop social skills, and make friends.

Children often talk of the pressure to be popular and to fit in, something often amplified by social media and its warped sense of success. Some children, again particularly those with SEN, can struggle with the growing requirement for independence and the busy school timetable. I remember a 13-year-old boy who had been taken out of mainstream school roll to be educated at home telling me it was OK at primary school because it was a small place and his teachers and school staff knew him personally and how he was. That all changed at secondary school, and he fell off the roll. There are plenty of good examples of transition programmes that support children from their final primary school years through the first years of secondary school, but once again there is no national template to reduce the disruption and cliff edges of transition. This is an area that the Government can be much more proactive on, drawing on best practice to produce a consistent plan that follows each child from primary to secondary, understands each child's needs, and provides the necessary help to support them.

Looking at a child's school life as one continuous journey should be an intrinsic part of our education system. Likewise, we should see schools as being there to offer children support and opportunities outside traditional school hours.

Whilst after-school and extracurricular activities do take place in most schools, the move to extend the school day has largely stalled since the demise of the extended schools programme over a decade ago. This is despite there being plenty of research showing that children from disadvantaged families benefit most from extracurricular activities.

These are the children who are much less likely to have access to sport, arts, or cultural pursuits, yet often they are unable to access facilities because they are locked behind a school gate. It's estimated that almost 40% of sports facilities in England sit in schools, and too often they go unused out of school hours. When you consider there is also a shortage of creative spaces for dance, arts, and music for young people, and the decrease in funding for youth activities, the argument that much more needs to be done with the school facilities we have beyond the traditional school day is compelling.

Police and community workers both tell me that levels of violence peak after schools close, causing a surge in demand on police time. Providing safe and stimulating places for children and young people to spend their time out of school offers protection, builds social networks and relationships with trusted adults, and gives them fun, stretching, and enjoyable things to do and take part in.

It is bizarre that we place so little emphasis on utilising school facilities as after-school assets for children. It makes no sense. These are buildings in every community, designed and built for children, full of resources for children, and so often closed at times that children need them. It's not about making schools or school staff do even more – it really is about opening up the precious resource to the community and inviting others to come in.

The best schools are already opening their doors before and after school, at weekends, and during school holidays. But it would make such a difference if there were funding so that all schools could do it, building a network of coaches, youth workers, specialists, and volunteers. It is no exaggeration to say that every parent I've ever asked about this reckons it makes sense. An initial amount of funding to adapt the building and prepare for extended opening would be a big step. Additional access doors so the school only has to open up in part, areas to socialise, and café areas – would be enough for some schools to start opening up when the classrooms close.

I've been impressed and inspired by schools I have visited that are not just places of learning but also the cornerstone of providing support to children and their families outside of core school hours. The Oasis Academy Hadley in Enfield has spent many years building relationships and trust with the local community so that there is a close bond between the school, with its bustling reception area open to parents to come in and chat or ask for advice, and the wider local community. Hadley's youth centre, with its incredible after-school facilities including sport, music, and discussion groups, sits next to the school geographically but it is also emotionally connected. Across the road is the Oasis family/community support centre, which provides help and advice to local families, including food, help with paying bills, advice and support with services, and community activities from early years onwards.

This joined-up, integrated offer to children and local families is a model for others to follow. Oasis Academy Hadley is providing a good education to children, not only through high academic and vocational ambitions and standards in the classroom but also by extending outwards beyond the classroom to become a key link between local partners, groups, and services.

Why can't all schools have this outward-looking focus, with a long-term vision, not just for academic achievement but also for the inclusive role the school can play in its local area?

It means building relationships and trust over a long period of time, looking ahead a decade or more to where the school will sit in its community, and deciding how the school will provide learning and support from the early years onwards, bringing together different agencies and expertise to meet the needs of every child from birth to 18.

I can't see why every school can't pick up this model and run with it. Community trust is built by making a school a key leader in bringing local support and services together, in the more formally recognised 'cradle-to-career' StriveTogether model.

StriveTogether is a movement developed initially in Cincinnati. Its purpose is to help every child succeed in school and in life. In partnership with communities across the US, it provides resources, best practices, and tools to create opportunities and to close gaps in education. Its cornerstone is an approach it calls its 'Theory of Action'. This model helps communities build and sustain the community infrastructure necessary to improve outcomes and close gaps from cradle to career.

Cradle-to-career partnerships are formal groups consisting of organisations and leaders from education, business, government, and third sector, as well as grassroots organisations, community leaders, and individuals from the local area. Members of the local community, particularly young people and their families, come together around a shared community vision. With support from 'backbone staff', the partnership group works together to define local challenges, to develop and implement strategies to address those challenges, and to hold systems accountable for results.

A shared community vision, evidence-based decision-making, collaborative action, investment and sustainability, and outcomes are at the heart of their work.

The StriveTogether model is the inspiration behind the Reach Academy, opened in 2012 to improve choice and opportunity for children and young people in Feltham. Compared with children in other parts of the London Borough of Hounslow, children growing up in Feltham are disproportionately affected by risk factors including parental stress, poor housing, multiple adverse childhood experiences, exclusion, poverty, poor mental health, poor diet, being academically behind more advantaged peers, lack of progress to a top university, living in an area lacking early years support, and fewer opportunities to enter the job market.

Reach has set out to tackle these disadvantages by opening a school that puts inclusivity, a rigorous curriculum, excellent teaching, and strong relationships at its heart. It is designed to ensure that all children are safe and well supported, are healthy, achieve well academically, and build strong relationships and social networks. Over the last ten years, Reach has achieved a 70% progress to higher education, a zero rate of young people not in education, employment, or training, and excellent GCSE results.

In 2018, it created a Children's Hub to complete its cradle-to-career model, setting up a pipeline of support for babies, children, and young people and their families that complements the work of the school and builds capacity within the local community. Reach believes that children do best when they grow up in an environment of nurturing relationships invested in their healthy development, and it builds trusted relationships through partnership across the community, providing strategic leadership to ensure children and their families receive the best possible support.

The Northern Powerhouse Partnership and the northern-focused education charity SHINE Trust think that the cradle-to-career model of schools is particularly relevant in tackling some of the north's more entrenched areas of disadvantage. SHINE has joined forces with partners across the public, private, and charity sector for a groundbreaking initiative to transform the lives of children and young people in the Merseyside community of North Birkenhead.

These models of community partnerships are showing how new approaches and partnerships can tear away the barriers for learning and life chances that are holding back so many children.

But this move towards an education system that values inclusion and supports vulnerable young people to succeed should not just be left to individual schools, local authorities, or academy trusts to develop in isolation. It should be part of the way we do things – and measured by the regulator Ofsted too.

This would be a big move. The main thrust in our education system through which children's 'success' is currently measured is based around progress and attainment. While that is important, focusing solely on these measures has serious limitations and can lead to the kinds of incentives to refuse admissions and overlook or exclude vulnerable children I set out earlier. Inclusion, effective and integrated specialist support, and 'alternative' provision within school, along with student wellbeing and community engagement, should be at the heart of what we judge to be a good school, alongside academic achievement and reflected in the measures that Ofsted are tasked with assessing.

Imagine the difference that inclusion and community engagement measures would make to incentivise schools to support more children to succeed. Organisations are already looking at how to develop a meaningful set of such inclusion measures of this kind – the difference would be transformational.

This should happen alongside a requirement for every school to publish its permanent and fixed-term exclusion rates every term, including for pupils with SEND and looked-after children, as well as the number of pupils who leave the school during the school year. This would really put the spotlight on educational excellence for all and introduce a new level of accountability for those schools that are consistently failing to provide an inclusive or supportive environment for the most vulnerable children.

There is also good practice that we could learn from some of the more inclusive colleges around the country. With over 60% of 16–19-year-olds attending a local college, and a disproportionate number of young people from disadvantaged backgrounds attending colleges, including children in care, this is a cohort that is more diverse and more likely to encounter adverse childhood experiences. It's striking how many young people who have been outside school and regular mainstream education during the secondary school years see going to college as a positive choice at 16. They talk of going to college as a new phase of their life – one that was more accessible, more about them as individuals, more about supporting their aspirations, and more about learning that will help them succeed in life. The potential for colleges to provide a springboard to success in adult life for the young people who have struggled in school is enormous.

The individual colleges I have spoken with and visited are often doing much more than school sixth forms to realise these ambitions, including identifying young people in need and providing support. There is a definite change in tone – inclusion by default. Colleges are more likely to have a wellbeing team and be very aware of contextual safeguarding, and will often be providing proactive education and information about staying safe. Many colleges have a more trauma-informed approach than many schools, backed up by staff training, as well as a greater commitment to tackling racism.

It is encouraging to see that many of the colleges in areas with serious violence hotspots are already working with their local VRUs. Others are seeking to build good relationships with children's services and the police – in some cases having onsite officers to build relationships with students. I've been impressed with how well some colleges gather the strategic information needed to map students in terms of those at potential risk through non-attendance, and how they see the link into exploitation. There is no reason why schools shouldn't be given the resources to do the same.

All professionals in and around college and schools want children to succeed. But let's remind ourselves, whilst most children do progress well in their education and have a positive experience of their school days, many don't. Remember that figure – a third of children leave school every year without basic qualifications. Thousands of children fall out of the education system every year through suspensions and permanent exclusions. A growing number of children, often children who need additional help that has not been provided, are being taken off the school roll to be educated at home without any adequate oversight of their safety or education outcomes. And the disproportionality of black children who are outside the mainstream, particularly black boys, is a shocking indictment of a system that is failing too many vulnerable children.

This is not what we should want for the young people of our country.

We don't want children as young as five experiencing multiple exclusions and being taken out of the mainstream system. Is this the best we can do? Surely, we have the expertise and creativity to find ways of helping support those children to overcome their difficulties.

We don't want young people falling out of mainstream education – their feelings of rejection, disappointment, embarrassment, and isolation – becoming frustrated and angry with a system that they feel can't or doesn't want to help them. We don't want some children to feel that school just isn't for people like them. Feeling that they are failures – which sometimes ends in catastrophe.

This does not have to be the case. But we have to choose to do things differently.

I have been bowled over by the schools that are working hard to help all their pupils succeed, with increasingly well-evidenced models. These schools are showing that starting early, working with children and their parents at the earliest opportunity to identify need and strengthen support, can have enormous impact. Building strong relationships, they stick with children, offering a continuum of education and support as they grow up. They work with parents to support children's needs beyond the school gate and help support them in class. They are ambitions and set sights high while understanding that many children need support at some stage of their school or college life, and so provide a focus on wellbeing and nurture as a standard for all children.

These schools work proactively to understand and respond to the deep-seated causes of problems rather than just reacting to the symptoms of problems they are presented with. They have built strong relationships with local services in the community so that waves of specialist help and support are available to children when it is needed. They hold on to and advocate for their children, understanding the importance of school in their lives and the protective factors it brings.

These schools are achieving remarkable things, and their leaders and teachers should be celebrated. For many of these schools, exclusions and children going off the roll just aren't part of their school life, and they are everything the culture and approach of their school is working against. School leaders have told me that they have taken this approach in the past because they know it is the right thing to do for their children and not because it is national policy. There is a sense that these schools have offered this inclusive approach despite a system that often seems incentivized to achieve the opposite. The system needs to catch up. Achieve for these children and you will achieve for all. It's what a good school system does and it's what a modern and ambitious country does.

Ultimately, a sea change towards inclusivity and community partnerships will require not just extra funding but a dramatic rethink of some of the cultures that have grown up in recent years. A new culture of inclusion is achievable, in my view, but must also run alongside providing schools and school leaders with the resources and national expectations for high levels of support for vulnerable children that partners can deliver.

We all want children to achieve academically, but there shouldn't be a trade-off between success for most and a significant proportion of children underachieving. We have to develop an education system that encourages and rewards the success of all children. I'd like to see transitional funding to pump-prime local authority area-wide inclusion strategies and to provide support packages for schools that include therapeutic support staff, education psychologists, family workers, youth workers, and mental health support.

We need new innovations, new community partnerships, and new data initiatives to nurture excellence in support for children with SEN, for children at risk of falling out of school, and for ambitious new approaches such as 'cradle to career'.

Let's focus on those places where communities are struggling and bring together academia, education, business, government, grassroots and community organisations, community leaders, and charities to work together to define local challenges, develop long-term strategies for growth, and bring about real change.

Let's have a national debate about what we want from our

schools and communities, and task and fund our public services and regulators to make it happen.

Let's value inclusion and make school league tables include it and wellbeing, alongside exam results.

Most parents would welcome these moves wholeheartedly. Of course, they want a local school to help their children pass exams, but they also want to be assured that their child's school is willing to stick with them and provide extra support if needed, and is not going to try and move their child off the school roll at the first sign of challenging behaviour.

At a time when finances are tight, the reality is that new money will be needed. But this is sound investment that has the potential to fuel economic growth, improving skills and the nation's pro-ductivity. The introduction of the pupil premium – extra money provided to schools by government to help disadvantaged pupils – over the last decade was a welcome acknowledgement that some children need to receive extra funding, but it needs to become a more dynamic catalyst for social mobility – and it needs to extend to older disadvantaged pupils – 16–19-year-olds.

I don't believe for a moment that schools can solve all society's problems by themselves, but I do believe they can be the catalyst and gateway for children to succeed – and that means all chil-dren. There are already local inclusion strategies in some areas that support a local exploitation and reduction of harm plan as part of community safety and as part of a wider wellbeing plan. I would like all areas to build inclusive schools into their health and wellbeing plans and wider community safety initiatives. In turn, support agencies should be working alongside local charities and community organisations to deliver support in and around schools.

Vulnerable children are more likely to fall through the gaps in all these services, and only by services working together can this be prevented. That means requiring schools to be part of the local child safeguarding partnership and putting a new responsibility on local child safeguarding partnerships to publish an annual school inclusion and prevention plan focusing on children at risk of violence or crime.

I would also like to see new local partnerships between education, children's services, and health to ensure that children who need support to learn get the help they need at the right time. This would include support delivered as part of an EHCP but also support for children with lower-level SEN and/or autism. An enhanced Designated Health Officer would work in every local authority, ensuring the system was operating effectively and that schools and pupils had the support they need to ensure children remained in their school and were able to learn. Health teams would work with schools to deliver education psychologists and therapeutic support as well as mental health support.

The next chapter will look at how to provide better mental health support for children at school and how to promote the development of a whole-school approach to mental wellbeing.

I would also like to see teams of youth and community workers in all schools to build relationships and support young people. These would be vital in supporting children back into school who are not attending. School-based family workers, working alongside and as part of the supporting families' teams and liaising with children's centres, family hubs, and children's services, would make a huge difference to supporting and strengthening those families where there are risks children will fall out of school or into exploitation or the criminal justice system.

Just as I want to reduce the chance of vulnerable children falling through the gaps in services by building strong local partnerships, we must reduce the chances of children falling behind or out of their education as the system changes through transitions.

Our education system should be a continuum of learning, from the earliest days of life through school and then on to a career.

This personalised learning would allow for the education journey to follow children's development and would be informed by an early identification of needs. It would be supported by a continuum of support from trusted organisations and services and be backed up by a consistent personal identification number . Given the link between children's health, educational, and social outcomes, it would make sense that data collected on children is shared between different agencies. Giving every child a unique consistent identification number would give professionals working with children the ability to share information far more easily and so improve care and outcomes.

The Start for Life scheme has huge potential and should be extended to every area in the country. It should be able to respond to additional needs of children and their families from conception into the first years of life, wherever they are growing up. It can be delivered through family hubs, building on the children's centres that we lost over the last decade. This could provide a particular focus on family vulnerability – parental mental health, domestic violence, and addiction, as well as wider issues of poor housing and poverty. Support in the first years of life would form the basis of a continuum of support throughout the childhood.

I would like to see a new school readiness programme that brings together education and health in a combined programme to increase the number of children starting school meeting their development goals. This would include the provision of speech and language support for every child who that needs it, rather than the postcode lottery we have now. Personalised and family support should be available throughout primary and secondary years as part of inclusive schools.

We also need to give every child a positive vision of life beyond school. That means much better and much earlier career and employment education, a focus on employment tasters, and clearer skills and employment pathways for all children. There should be a new focus on pathways to employment with a guarantee of high-quality internships for disadvantaged students – funded and supported by a partnership between business and the Department for Business, Innovation and Skills.

We should be encouraging and supporting schools to embrace arts, design, music, communication, digital, artificial intelligence (AI), and publishing, and making new creative content and approaches that can engage and inspire young people in a way that reflects the creativity they enjoy as standard outside classroom and in their digital world.

The alternative is to continue to lose the talent of thousands of young people every year who are smart and creative and have so much to offer but are often drifting out of AP without opportunities. We need to harness those talents to create a new generation of high achievers, and divert children away from crime, exploitation, and serious violence.

So, I would like to see the development of a new 'Creating to Achieve' curriculum programme that embraces, engages, and inspires young people to gain the skills needed in the workforce of tomorrow. We could even levy a charge on tech companies to fund Specialist Creative Programmes, backed and designed in partnership with the creative industries to run in schools and specialist schools.

It is important to repeat that schools alone cannot keep every child safe. But we could be doing so much more to prevent children falling into danger because they are not in school. We shouldn't have a situation where schools don't focus on vulnerable children because they don't feel they have an obligation or responsibility to do so. We shouldn't be praising and rewarding schools that aren't willing to stick with children through thick and thin, or that don't feel it is in the school's interest to even have vulnerable children there at all.

We can have an education system that inspires all children, that understands the needs of all children as individuals, and that supports and works with them and their families and local community to help them to succeed.

We can encourage an educational experience where learning is a part of a deep relationship lasting from cradle to career and not just a temporary transaction.

We can intervene to help those children who are struggling to adapt or when a child's circumstances change.

Childhood comes in different waves, and so should support at school, and we can make these changes if, as a society, we choose to do so.

CHAPTER 7

Boosting Mental Health

Not long ago, I was talking with a friend who is a school leader, someone who is responsible for thousands of children across a large academy chain. While we were speaking, he received a call on his mobile from one of his headteachers to tell him that a teenage student had taken her own life. I was stunned. I assumed that such a terrible event must be unusual, happening only a handful of times in the career of a school leader.

In fact, I was wrong. My friend told me that teenagers attempting to take their own life, sometimes fatally, was now happening regularly in many schools, particularly since the Covid pandemic. While he was extremely upset, my friend was not shocked. This was now part and parcel of running schools, and of many young people's lives.

A few days later, I was visiting a college in the north of England, also part of a group of further education colleges with a large cohort. I met their brilliant student welfare team, dedicated professionals in their 20s and 30s who were providing support to hundreds of young people, some of them experiencing very serious mental health conditions. As well as sharing their experiences of how Covid had hit many of their students, they also talked about the general rise in mental health issues among the young people with whom they worked, starting from well before the pandemic.

I was particularly struck by their sense of dread as the upcoming Easter holidays were approaching. Previously during the spring break, there had been a spike in suicide attempts among their students.

Over the last few years, these stories have become too familiar. One of the first conversations I had with a young person after my appointment as Children's Commissioner was about mental health. She told me that she had only been able to access children's mental health services after she attempted suicide. The bar for referrals was so high, and the waiting lists for treatment so long, that she felt this was her only option. It is an experience I have heard from other young people, and their families, many times since.

In fact, it is hard to recall a teacher, youth worker, or anyone working in children's services who has responded positively when I have asked them about the mental health and wellbeing of the young people they are working with.

Just as Covid has rocket boosted other vulnerabilities, so it has for young people's mental health. Every day I hear about the children who have hardly returned to school since 2020, the increase in the regularity and extreme nature of young people's mental health problems, the stories of self-harm, and suicide attempts. The chief executive officer of the world leading South London and Maudsley NHS Foundation Trust told the BBC in 2022 that 200 young people are now attending A&E departments in London every week after trying to take their own life.[1]

The scale of the problem has forced policymakers and the Government to confront the long-standing inadequacy of children's mental health services over the last few years. When in 2017, as

---

1   Interview on: The World at One, 25 July 2022, BBC Radio 4.

Children's Commissioner, I published a report very critical of the state of children's mental health services, the initial response from the Government and the NHS was to question the scale of the problem. That doesn't happen anymore. We all now know that it is bad and that Covid has made it worse.

The pandemic really was a disaster for the mental health of many children. Thousands of young people are still struggling with its after-effects. One in six children in England aged 6–16 were identified as having a probable mental health problem in July 2021, a huge increase from the already troubling one in nine in 2017.[2]

In March 2022, over 90,000 young people were referred to NHS Children and Young People's Mental Health Services (CYPMHS), the highest figure since the measure first began being collected. There was an increase of almost 50% in the number of new emergency referrals to crisis care teams in under-18s between December 2019 and April 2021. It has been estimated that 1.5 million children and young people in England will need either new or additional mental health support following the pandemic.[3]

These numbers are enormous, yet I don't find them surprising. Speaking with young people about how Covid impacted on their mental health, I've heard them talk about feeling lonely, how some felt they had to relearn social skills, and how school often felt overwhelming for the first time.

For some young people, Covid had affected their ability to learn and their willingness to be in school, and had triggered or exacerbated mental health struggles they were already having before the pandemic. Some children told me they spent two years feeling scared during the repeated lockdowns.

---

2   Survey conducted in July 2020 shows one in six children having a probable mental disorder, 2020, NHS Digital.

3   Covid-19 and the nation's mental health: May 2021, 2021, Centre for Mental Health.

Before Covid, we were starting to move in the right direction. New funding commitments to improve NHS CYPMHS were put forward as part of the NHS 'Long Term Plan'. Children's mental health services have widened, there is more early help in schools, and there has been an increase in spending and in access to support.

Yet the number of children suffering with mental health conditions continues to rise, waiting lists for CYPMHS are sky high, and most schools still do not have adequate counselling and other support in place to make early interventions.

Fewer than a quarter of children who are referred to services start treatment within the four-week waiting target, and we're still spending much less on children's mental health than we spend on adult mental health.

In a survey carried out by Young Minds in 2022,[4] more than one in four young people with mental health problems said they had tried to take their own life while having to wait for support. More than four in ten waited more than a month for mental health support after seeking it, and almost one in ten were turned away.

We know that the teenagers most at risk of violence and harm have high levels of mental health need, often undiagnosed and often exacerbated by the trauma they experience at home or in other settings. These factors increase their vulnerability at a time when many are already under severe pressure. Children who end up in custody are three times more likely to have mental health problems than those who do not.

Minoritised Ethnic communities are over-represented for certain mental health difficulties, and some children say that they are put off by a negative perception towards support and care, limited and involuntary pathways to mental health services, a lack of

---

4   Mental health waiting times harming young people, n.d., YoungMinds.

mental health awareness, a lack of culturally appropriate support, and mental health stigma.

Children and young people with SEND and their families are also at greater risk of experiencing poor mental health. NHS Digital data suggests more than half of 6–16-year-olds with SEND have a probable mental disorder, compared with just over one in ten without SEND.

Then there is the dysfunctional care system. Overall, half of all children in care meet the criteria for a possible mental health disorder. They are more likely to have experienced trauma and negative childhood experiences, which can have detrimental impacts on a child's mental health. They are also more likely to have been exposed to adversity in childhood, to have been exploited and in need of more acute care, and to experience instability whilst in care. Those who are sent long distances 'out of area' can see relationships with their friends and families break down, which can have a deep and negative impact on their mental health and sense of worth.

As I have already argued, falling out of school through exclusion puts some children at greater risk of harm. Often that process of being excluded from school is accompanied by mental health problems or triggered by them. Even before Covid, many young people with mental health conditions found secondary school a challenge. They were more likely to be excluded, to miss school altogether, and to have poorer academic outcomes.

Almost every teacher or member of teaching staff I have spoken to over the last two years has talked about how the mental health of their students worsened during lockdown. The loss of routine, social isolation, and struggle to access support all contributed to feelings of anxiety, stress, and depression.

It is so obvious to anyone working with children with mental health conditions that their health cannot be taken in isolation, and that the above factors and others, like temporary housing, growing up in poverty, and living in homes with parents who have mental health problems or addictions or where there is domestic violence, can have a hugely detrimental impact on a young person's mental health.

So many of those who enter prison and the criminal justice system do so with a history of trauma, abuse, substance misuse, and poor mental health. These children are also more likely to have more than one mental health problem, have a learning difficulty, be dependent on drugs and alcohol, and to have experienced other serious life challenges. While the NHS has committed to improving care for young people with complex needs by placing trauma-informed and integrated services at the heart of its plans, as yet, what this means in practice is sketchy.

Unsurprisingly, the rising tide of mental health needs and vulnerability to exploitation and crime are interlinked, and far too often children are more likely to be locked up because of a failure to provide them with the right support before they reach crisis point and commit a crime.

One in three children in prison have mental health difficulties and many of the mental health needs of those most at risk of offending are not being recognised or met by existing services.

I believe this deterioration in the mental health of so many of our young people, combined with a mental health support system still not able to cope with demand or reach all of those who need it, is a huge generational threat to our nation's future national prosperity and success. It comes on the back of a once-in-a-generation pandemic event, which is why we need a once-in-a-generation package of support to make our mental health services for children fit for purpose.

As everyone working with young people at risk knows, when we fail as a society to protect children in care, or children who

have fallen through gaps in the family support or education systems, we boost the chances of those resourceful, manipulative,
and ruthless criminals and abusers. Children who are suffering
from untreated or inadequately supported mental health conditions and trauma are often falling through the same gaps too and
into the same danger. Often their mental health conditions are a
precursor to the horrific situations they find themselves in as victims of criminal or sexual exploitation.

That is why we need a much better focus on prevention, on
intervening to identify and respond to poor mental health when
it does occur, and on delivering long-term support through help
and services that are accessible.

In 2022, Integrated Care Systems, including Integrated Care
Boards responsible for planning and funding most NHS services
in an area, were created as legal entities with statutory powers and
responsibilities to bring together local authorities and the NHS
to plan care and to increase the availability of mental health and
wellbeing support in schools and colleges. This is an opportunity
to drive change and make sure local services work more closely
with the people they are there to support. Most aren't delivering
for children and young people in the way they could yet – but the
potential to develop a joined-up system of support is one that we
should take.

Since 2018, there has been the roll-out of Mental Health Support Teams in schools and colleges, and training for a new senior
mental health lead in every school and college. They are well regarded and showing signs of success for those children with mild
to moderate mental health problems. In 2022, almost 2.5 million
children in England had access to a mental health team in their
school or college.

But they need to be in all schools, and they need the money
behind them to make sure that they become a permanent feature.

It is the speed and scale of this roll-out that concerns me. The current trajectory means that two out of three schools and colleges will have no mental health team in place from this programme by the middle of this decade, leaving most young people without the help they need in school.

A theme throughout this book is the need for services and support that can respond early to problems. When it comes to children's mental health, this isn't happening in vast swathes of the country. CYPMHS are underfunded and don't have the workforce in place to meet demand.

Early evaluation of the mental health teams in schools[5] has also found that some of the most vulnerable young people, and those with more complex needs are not accessing support from the CYPMHS – the part of the system that is meant to deliver specialist treatment for those with more serious mental health treatment. Going back to what young people have told me over the last decade about not being able to get this kind of help, this shouldn't be a surprise, but it happens so often because there just isn't enough of the right kind of support to go around. Clinical thresholds are too high and too rigid as a result. It's also the case that when young people have a wide range of problems that may not be extreme in any one area, they often aren't 'ill enough' to meet any one of the thresholds, meaning they don't get treated even though all the problems together are having a very negative effect.

Of course, when children don't get the help they need, the problems don't go away. Far from it – they will often escalate. These children can then ricochet around services, not receiving the help they need until they hit crisis point. The reality is that because young people with complex, less well-understood difficulties do

---

5   Early evaluation of the Children and Young People's Mental Health Trailblazer programme, 2021, Ellins, J. et al.

not fit clearly into diagnostic boxes, some are at risk of not being able to access NHS specialist support at all. This is a problem affecting tens of thousands of children and driving crisis.

> I have heard too many harrowing examples of young people who have attempted suicide but have still not been able to access support from their CYPMHS. I was told about a teenage boy who was discharged from hospital after trying to take his own life, but after ten days nobody from mental health services had been in touch. Another teenage girl admitted to A&E by ambulance following a suicide attempt was discharged 12 hours later and, despite her family contacting mental health services every day for over a week, did not receive any follow-up or even a phone call.

These are not isolated cases – they are becoming more normal. I have even heard how some services are now only taking on young people after two suicide attempts.

At the same time, many of those who do receive some support find clinical settings alienating. Some young people say that they are not turning up for appointments because they are being asked to attend somewhere that doesn't feel right for them or at a time during the school day that doesn't work for them. There are huge issues with getting some young people in front of a professional.

Indeed, it is clear from the young people and professionals I speak with that mental health services as they are currently being delivered are just not working for many of the most marginalised, vulnerable teenagers – the children often most at risk of exploitation or becoming involved in the criminal justice system.

They tell me that services feel stigmatising, traumatic, and even as if they are being criminalised.

These negative perceptions of mental health services come

about for a range of reasons, often because young people them-selves have previously had bad experiences of statutory services, including those who have experienced racism.

Those least likely to receive treatment are males aged 16–24 from minority communities. Just as the teaching workforce is overwhelmingly white, so is the clinical psychology workforce. Support services are also often seen as lacking cultural sensitivity and not being representative of the communities they work with.

These communities are more likely to report more dissatisfaction with mainstream mental health care, and so, unsurprisingly, they often don't engage. They are then labelled as hard to reach, when it is the services that are not reaching out to them. I've even heard some communities described as those that the system finds most challenging. Having the will to understand what kinds of services are needed and how they can most effectively be delivered would be a good starting point.

This disproportionate failure of mental health services to support many young black teenagers joins the evidence of failure in the school and care systems to deliver interventions before moments of crisis set out earlier in this book.

If you are young and black, you are less likely to access services early, so are more likely to experience the crisis end of the spectrum. This shows in stark statistics – young black men are more likely to be detained under the Mental Health Act, and black children are ten times more likely to be referred to CYPMHS via social services rather than through a GP, compared with white British children.[6]

Black people are also 40% more likely to access treatment through a police or criminal justice route, less likely to receive

---

6   Racial disparities in mental health: literature and evidence review, 2019, Race
     Equality Foundation.

psychological therapies, more likely to be compulsorily admitted for treatment, more likely to be on a medium or high secure ward, and more likely to be subject to seclusion or restraint. It's all there for us to see.

Going to a treatment centre and being prescribed a programme of clinical treatment, even with the best intentions, can be overwhelming, uncomfortable, and overly medicalised for many young people. For the generation used to a fast-moving digital world, the whole system can seem completely out of date and archaic.

Young people will often say that they want to go to places they know and trust to get help, where they feel safe and where support is something they feel part of and not being 'done to them'. They want a place where they can express themselves without judgement and they want people they trust and can relate to working with them.

This distrust is shared by their families too. As previous chapters have highlighted, many of the most vulnerable families have a deep distrust of bureaucratic statutory services already, fearful that they will be labelled as 'bad parents' and judged. These parents say they want non-judgemental care in a community environment they trust.

That is why we need to expand the models of support available to young people and their families, and to fund them properly.

There are already many great examples across the country of local services, organisations, and schools that are providing consistency of engagement, working with both parents and children together, building confidence, focusing on human and relational approaches, and ensuring inclusivity in a way that can really boost young people's mental health.

I have found it fascinating to hear young people talking about what they would like from mental health services. So often it mirrors what schools, mental health campaigners and service providers, practitioners, and experts are proposing.

Solutions cannot just be clinical – they must also be holistic and wide-ranging.

Teenagers I speak with talk about how they want to be able to build relationships with people they know and trust, how youth clubs, sports and arts groups, and drop-in centres are preferable to speaking about very personal issues with a random stranger. Finding ways to work with young people in surroundings and contexts that are meaningful to them must be at the heart of rebuilding a children's mental health service that is fit for purpose.

There is no doubt that young people themselves want to be involved in activities that improve their own wellbeing. When asked what that might be, they will often say sport, art, drama, volunteering – activities that involve socialising and communicating, that build a shared experience, and as one teenager put it, that can get you 'out of yourself' and into a space where you are thinking about other things and other people.

There is a growing consensus that developing opportunities to build trusted relationships and working with local organisations to build activities and support, giving them continuity and certainty, is the future.

For example, in Dorset, there is a focus on funding 'navigators' to develop and maintain relationships with families and children. Much of the work is holistic and avoids families having to work with an overwhelming array of different individuals and service providers. The work takes a trauma-informed approach, recognising that mental health is not exclusively the domain of health and secondary care services.

Barnardo's Core Priority Programme in mental health and wellbeing puts early intervention and prevention at its core. It has developed a strategic partnership with North Tyneside council to co-design, test, and implement different approaches to support-ing young people's mental health. The partnership is exploring system transformation following a process of local discovery of what the context, strengths, and challenges are in that local area, with pilots to test out what works. They have identified a gap in the knowledge of education staff in the area around mental health and wellbeing. As a result, North Tyneside has chosen to focus on in-vesting in a programme of capacity building in schools by training staff in Mental Health First Aid. The aim is to build a more focused whole-school approach to mental health and wellbeing.

Services delivered in the community can provide cost-effective support while reaching underserved communities and offering a less stigmatising, more culturally responsive approach. This in turn can reduce referrals to more expensive specialist support, freeing up capacity and budgets.

The Premier League funds a major national programme called Kicks, which is delivered by football clubs to engage and support young people from disadvantaged communities. Reading FC is one club that offers community-based, structured activities to young people through the programme. Sessions are open to men-tal health professionals – again, as a way of building trust and re-lationships.

Similarly, London Youth's 'Good for Girls' programme sup-ports young women to access holistic early intervention for men-tal health support in trusted community spaces. Youth clubs are supported to become mental health hubs where trained profes-sionals can create safe spaces where young women can talk about their mental health and learn how to manage their wellbeing.

The Nest, which is based in the London Borough of Southwark, is a youth-centred service that also offers early intervention and prevention for emotional issues, as well as low-level mental health concerns. It is available at the point of need, without the need for a professional referral, and provides young people and families with the opportunities, experiences, and tools to enable them to develop their physical, emotional, and social capabilities.

Its non-clinical interventions offer youth work, person-centred counselling, psychological wellbeing practices, and traditional talking therapies via one-to-one sessions, group work, virtual resources, and peer mentoring.

It has a regular programme of drop-in sessions for children, young people, and their families to speak to a member of staff without the need for an appointment and has embedded a wide system of support for young people in Southwark, developing links with family support, schools, CYPMHS, GPs, social services, and the nearby Goldsmith's University.

The Nest has also worked with the Mayor's Office for Policing and Crime (MOPAC) and the council's early help team to develop a parent-champion network to encourage and empower parents to deliver peer-to-peer support. The Parent Champion I met could hardly get to the school gate for parents wanting to chat and get advice.

A lot of energy goes into reaching out to young people, and in schools, Nest delivers support through assemblies, workshops for students, and staff training. This has a direct impact on who walks through its doors and asks for help. Most referrals to the Nest are from young people themselves, and two thirds of the referrals are people from Minoritised Ethnic backgrounds, mirroring Southwark's demographic makeup and highlighting how community-based trusted organisations and programmes can break down the barriers preventing some communities from seeking help.

It is an excellent template for other services to follow.

The growth of these kinds of community drop-in mental health hubs over recent years has been a hugely positive development. They can be a really important place for improving young people's access to early help in the community, offering easy-to-access, drop-in support on a self-referral basis. Often delivered in partnership between the NHS, local authorities, and the voluntary sector, they can reduce pressures on NHS services and offer space to access more flexible support.

Youth Information Advice and Counselling Services are already providing help to thousands of young people with comparable clinical outcomes to NHS CYPMHS and school-based counselling and can also be an effective gateway to more specialist support.

The think tank Centre for Mental Health has estimated that a national network of hubs would cost approximately £103 million a year and would be able to help around half a million children. Having a hub like this in your local area would transform the opportunities for so many young people to get help. It's good to see that some politicians are catching on to this and it would be great to see them become reality.

The role of 'social prescribing' has also become more prominent in recent years. It involves helping patients to improve their mental health and wellbeing by connecting them to activities or community organisations that can help improve their wellbeing. Schemes can often include providing arts, sport, youth clubs, or physical activities.

There is plenty of evidence to back up the positive impact social prescribing can have on health and wellbeing outcomes, and it seems to be particularly effective for disadvantaged young people.

I visited the First Class Foundation in Birmingham, which is challenging the over-representation and under-representation of Minoritised Ethnic young people in key sectors including mental health, criminal justice, and education. They told me how, often, if a young black person is going through mental health problems and they go and see a GP, that GP will usually prescribe them medication. What if instead they prescribed them some music sessions, some talking sessions, a fitness boot camp? Other organisations have told me how the NHS is now asking them to make interventions with young people at risk, like walk and talks in the park – on the one hand, simply having a chat and a stroll, but in reality, providing an informal therapeutic intervention.

Social prescribing for children and young people is still in its infancy but plenty of good practice has already emerged. Stort Valley and Villages Primary Care Network has developed a children and young people's social prescribing programme to reduce the number of young people being referred to specialist services. Its programme is a patient-centred, non-medicalised approach to improving wellbeing and mental health, with a children and young person's social prescriber building connections with local services such as schools and activity-based groups. Patients aged 11–25 years old are offered up to six one-to-one sessions with the social prescriber to create a personalised care plan.

The service is supported by a multidisciplinary team who provide support with referrals and cases, and who are supported by a GP clinical supervisor who can discuss cases and will see any patient referred by the team. They seek to engage with parents whenever possible, and a mental health coach provides sessions for parents to educate them on supporting their children with their mental health.

Inevitably, the pandemic saw a rise in the use of digital support to help young people with their mental health, and there is a growing consensus that this method can have many benefits, including giving young people more choice in how they access support and a greater degree of anonymity. Services like Kooth, an online anonymous service that offers online counselling sessions, and is commissioned by the NHS, councils, charities, and businesses, is providing support to thousands of young people already.

Its live counselling services allow young people to receive professional support through either booked or drop-in sessions. It also offers a range of services that young people can pick and choose, allowing them to decide what help they want – be that magazines, forums, activities, or counselling.

Kooth is immediate and there is no need for a referral, there are no waiting lists, and the service is always available.

As these chapters have already said, the role of schools and colleges in a young person's life cannot be overestimated, and education settings should play a crucial role in supporting mental health and wellbeing.

Research shows that if a child feels like they belong in a school and are being listened to, they are more likely to have a positive attitude to seeking support for mental health needs. Whole-school approaches, where the school promotes wellbeing and positive mental health, can have a huge impact on young people's experiences, and there has been a growing recognition of the importance of this approach.

Place2Be provides embedded mental health services in hundreds of primary and secondary schools already. It takes a whole-school approach like this, by embedding therapeutic mental health support in schools and aiming to strengthen the system around the child by also offering support to families and school staff through a range of targeted and universal interventions. Support is offered via one-to-one counselling sessions and online parenting courses, and to school staff via training.

Place2Be is reaching some of the most vulnerable young people – it says 46% of those who use its one-to-one service are receiving free school meals, 25% are involved with social care, 8% were the subject of a child protection plan, and 38% had four or more adverse childhood experiences such as abuse, domestic violence, or loss of a parent.

Its evidence also suggests that almost eight out of ten of those with severe difficulties showed an improvement in their mental health and that the benefits of its service can reduce rates of absenteeism, smoking, exclusion, depression, and crime.

Similarly, the Compass BUZZ project, which runs across all 400 schools in North Yorkshire, is also supporting school leaders, teachers, and pastoral staff to gain the knowledge and skills to support the mental health of their pupils and staff through direct interventions based on a whole-school approach.

Services that place the role of the trusted adult and relationships at the centre of the work they do are also making a difference. Football Beyond Borders works with young people from areas of socio-economic disadvantage who are passionate about football but disengaged from school to help them finish school with the skills and grades to make a successful transition to adulthood.

It provides long-term, intensive support built around relationships and has been piloting a therapeutic offer to the most at-risk participants. It has developed culturally competent, highly skilled therapists and counsellors as part of its school programme and has offered support to over 250 young people over the last three years.

In Greater Manchester, funded by the Home Office's Trusted Relationships Fund, psychologists are being integrated into Complex Safeguarding teams working with children affected by extra-familial abuse, in particular child sexual exploitation and child criminal exploitation. They work with multi-agency professionals to support trauma-informed practice and offer a bespoke child-centred approach. The Trusted Relationship role provides psychological case consultations, bespoke staff training, and staff support.

Alongside this community-based support, we need a mental

health services system that provides more targeted support to those at risk of offending.

The Youth Justice Service (YJS) works with children aged 10–18 who have been sentenced by a court or who have come to the attention of the police because of their offending behaviour, and typically has a co-located or seconded NHS children and young people mental health specialist working with its teams. Some teams also have other health specialists such as speech and language therapists.

This enables an assessment of underlying health and neurodevelopmental needs as an offending risk factor. YJS tries to divert children and young people away from the court and the criminal justice system so their health needs can be addressed without unnecessarily criminalising the child.

Cheshire YJS provides a child-centred diversionary scheme to prevent and divert children away from the criminal justice system when a primary contributor to their offending is a previously unmet health need. Health issues are screened and fully assessed at the point of arrest as opposed to the point of sentence for children and young people across the Cheshire region, so young people with underlying or previously undiagnosed health conditions or SEND are diverted away from the criminal justice system into more appropriate treatment pathways.

These programmes are producing encouraging results. The Divert scheme in Cheshire and similar schemes run by YJS across the country have reduced the number of 'first-time' entrants into the criminal justice system. The Children's Society Climb service, a diversionary service funded by West Mercia Police and Crime Commissioner, works with young people aged 10–17 who are missing school or college, starting to be reported as missing, or at risk of being drawn into criminal activity. It offers sport, dance, arts, music, and other activities to young people to help them build their resilience and keep them safe from harm.

Project Future is a community-based, youth-led project, that seeks to transform mental health delivery for young men aged 16–25 who are involved in offending and serious youth violence in Haringey, London. The project is funded by the Big Lottery Fund and has been co-produced alongside young men in the community, underpinned by the ethos that they are experts in their own lives and are best placed to know what would support their community.

It is staffed by a team of clinical psychologists, specialist youth workers and local young people, and 'community consultants' who provide a supportive and nurturing environment for young people. It is perceived by its users to be somewhere that makes them feel respected, safe, accepted, empowered, and supported.

There is also positive practice happening through VRUs. The Lancashire VRU is instilling trauma-informed practice into its culture, and Thames Valley VRU is implementing a Sequential Intercept Model (SIM) as a framework for addressing children and young people with neurodevelopmental disorders and disabilities in contact with the criminal justice system because of violence. The SIM can illustrate key stages where intervention can prevent the current status quo of young people with neurodevelopmental disorders being over-represented in custody.

The Your Choice programme delivered by London's VRU offers intensive, therapeutic support for young people aged 11–17 who are at most risk of being affected by violence or exploitation. Specialist frontline practitioners deliver Cognitive Behavioural Therapy to help young people.

Commissioned by Thames Valley VRU, the Navigator Programme, delivered by Starting Point, works with those aged 13–24 who attend A&E for violence-related injuries and/or risk-taking behaviour. The Navigators have conversations and connect with young people in A&E and then work with them to help them access additional support in the community, including offering long-term mentoring support.

These community-based approaches to supporting the mental health needs of marginalised and excluded groups of young people show that when services provide support in the community, through trusted organisations, those who are often unfairly labelled as 'hard to reach' will become involved.

Voluntary sector organisations working in the community are serving a greater proportion of teenagers and young people from Minoritised Ethnic communities. Going to the barber shop can feel like a much safer environment than a statutory service clinic. Professionals with 'lived experience' are also too often undervalued, despite the evidence showing that these are the people who can often best bridge the gap between services and those who use them.

Partisan is a culturally sensitive organisation that is representative of the communities it works with. Based outside of clinics, its team of psychotherapists and clinical and community psychologists work on the ground with children, young people, families, and communities. They have a highly flexible approach and believe in sharing ideas and good practice with others who have relationships with people in their communities. Most of their work is in black communities, and many of the people they work with have been affected by violence, exploitation, poverty, and racial trauma.

Partisan has developed a new partnership with Lewisham Council and local community organisations to give culturally sensitive wellbeing and mental health support in safe and accessible community locations. It co-develops bespoke mental health and wellbeing support with community champions, working alongside them to integrate psychologically and trauma-informed approaches into their existing work.

The INTEGRATE approach, developed by MAC-UK in partnership with excluded young people, seeks to wrap holistic and responsive support, including mental health and emotional wellbeing provision, around excluded young people.

The model was first developed in Camden in 2007 with the founding principle that services need to meet young people where they are at. INTEGRATE teams are led by mental health professionals and made up of workers with lived experience and other professional staff, such as youth workers, all trained in mental health. They have been successful in engaging with groups of young people who are engaged with or at risk of offending behaviour.

All these programmes and initiatives are delivering services differently and making sure that young people are receiving support in their community with people they trust and feel they are given some control.

The organisations and programmes are bursting with life and potential for a new approach to support young people to stay well. Government and the NHS need to better understand how important these approaches are and to be much bolder in rolling them out nationally as part of a new system of support. The young people most at risk of exploitation or serious violence are so often not the ones who will self-diagnose mental health difficulties or self-refer themselves for treatment and help. They need mental health support that seeks them out, delivers in a way that meets their needs in the community, and is there for the long term. Let's make co-production and community work a cornerstone of mental health care.

I want to see a national social prescription scheme in every area that enables GPs and health professionals to pay for sports, arts, music, drama, activities, youth clubs, and volunteering, and outlines how to improve young people's confidence and self-esteem.

It is a huge challenge to improve and transform services when you're in the middle of a crisis and the service is destabilised. How can the NHS possibly save the lives of 10,000 desperate children a year in our capital while it is struggling to meet the waiting times of just 20% of children?

Turning around CYPMHS will have to start with a significant long-term investment to guarantee appointment and treatment times, and I would like to see a national guarantee that all children and young people requiring specialist treatment be seen within a four-week period. This should include guaranteed next-day emergency appointments for children at risk of serious self-harm and suicide and should run alongside a serious commitment to increasing the participation and power of young people in decision-making about their care.

We should recognise and give credit to the Conservative Government and NHS England for the very real improvements that have been made over the last few recent years. The roll-out of mental health teams in schools has been very welcome. This well-evidenced programme is popular with children and school leaders and places children's mental health and wellbeing firmly at the heart of the school experience. Extending in-school mental health support should be a vital part of a long-term preventative approach to improve wellbeing and mental health.

The solutions to the growing mental health and wellbeing crisis need to be holistic. We need to start with a consistent approach where everyone who is going to work with a child and family prioritises wellbeing and supports good mental health. This means that integration of services and sharing knowledge and data is key, backed up by world-leading specialist treatment from children and young people's mental health support.

We also need to have guaranteed mental health assessments for children and young people at points of vulnerability. This would mean an automatic assessment and guaranteed mental health package for children entering care and automatic assessments for children and young people who are at risk of exclusion from school, go missing, are at the point of arrest, or are involved in violence or crime. It would include a guarantee of assessment by education psychologists for any child at risk of exclusion.

The many examples of good practice highlighted in this chapter need to be built on. I would like to see a much more ambitious programme of drop-in mental health hubs delivered in the community, and a national 'Programmes on Prescription' scheme in every area.

Delivering these improvements will also need a major recruitment programme with ambitious targets to build the children and young people workforce required to meet this expansion of services. It is vitally important to ensure that this workforce is diverse and culturally competent. We should also make sure wellbeing and mental health training and support is there for all professionals working with children and young people.

Finally, and another theme running through this book, there is the need to give better information and support to parents. So often they struggle to help their children with their mental health and do not know where to turn. I would like to see more resources for parents, and more support in schools, children's centres, and family hubs, to provide positive support to improve wellbeing and to find specialist help if needed.

The collapse in many of the family and youth support services that existed 10 or 20 years ago has left us playing catch-up when it comes to tackling the crisis in children's mental health. As one parent said to me recently, 'All the stuff that used to be there to stop things from happening isn't there anymore.'

We can start to rebuild 'all that stuff' – but in a different way – and rethink how we improve access to mental health support. The alternative is that we risk putting the post-Covid generation of vulnerable children in even greater danger of exploitation, abuse, and poor life chances.

CHAPTER 8

Being There to Care When Things Get Tough

Not all families will be able to keep children safe all the time, and there will always be the need for social care professionals to make swift, good judgements to provide alternative care when children are at risk of harm. Many family relationships have broken down by the time the decision to take the teenager into care is made. Months and months of grooming and exploitation as families are deliberately driven apart can often destroy relationships, and parents lose the battle to keep their children safe. Young people are taken into care to protect them from those who are seeking to exploit and harm them.

Teenagers have been the fastest growing group of children being taken into care over recent years and 16- and 17-year-olds now make up almost a quarter of the care population.[1] In March 2021, there were 80,850 children in care in England, a 1% rise on the year before and the highest on record.[2]

Young people in care are some of the brightest, most resilient people, with their whole future ahead of them. But they are having to live with some of the most challenging circumstances

---

[1] Characteristics of children entering care for the first time as teenagers, 2021, Children's Commissioner.

[2] Statistics: England: looked after children, adoption and fostering statistics for England, n.d., Coram Academy.

– domestic violence at home, neglect, and increasingly recognised over recent years, the danger of harm from outside the home – the risks posed by others who are looking to exploit – 'contextualised safeguarding' as it's called in social work jargon.

Being taken into care, with all the responsibilities of the state as corporate parent behind you, should be a sure way out of those difficulties, providing the love, stability, opportunities, and protection needed to recover and succeed. It sounds great, but unfortunately it's not like that for a lot of children in care.

Children in the care of the state do less well at school, are less likely to go to university, are more likely to be homeless in later life, and are more likely to end up in the criminal justice system. Figures released by the Office for National Statistics in 2022[3] show that children in care were much more at risk of being involved with the criminal justice system by the age of 24 than their peers. Over half (52%) of the care experienced children had been convicted of a criminal offence by the academic year they turned 24. Our care system is not protecting our young people and it is happening in plain sight.

There is also much to be done to specifically investigate the experience of black boys and girls at risk and identify where there is racial bias in our systems. It is very evident that community-based, black-led services that work closely with the growing number of black boys on the edge of care and within the system have a huge role to play – to support families, prevent children getting into danger, and improve the care system.

I have no doubt that the children's social care system is letting down many Minoritised Ethnic children. Just as these children are over-represented in the criminal justice system, so they are

---

3   The education background of looked-after children who interact with the criminal justice system, 2022, Office for National Statistics.

over-represented in the care system. We know too that there was a 33% drop in the number of mixed background and black children adopted between 2015 and 2019.[4]

Anyone who takes a closer look will quickly see that the current children's social care system is not serving vulnerable teenagers well, whether they are on the edge of care and at risk of exploitation and violence or experiencing severe harm.

A care system that was largely designed for young children has struggled to adapt to the needs of older children. There is a chronic lack of appropriate foster homes for teenagers and not enough residential places. Where there are residential places, they are often far from home, isolating young people from their family, friends, school, and support network.

The shortage of residential places means that thousands of young people don't get the care they need; instead, they are sent to semi-independent accommodation with only support services for back up. Still loosely regulated with new national standards, semi-independent placements can be very variable in quality, with many young people complaining of dirty, dangerous, and unfit accommodation that makes them feel unsafe and a target for adults who want to sell them drugs and alcohol or exploit them. By 2021, the number of 16- and 17-year-olds in unregulated care had fallen slightly to 5,980, having more than doubled from 2013–2020. Just over three quarters were aged 17 in the settings which, since September 2021, have been barred to children aged under 16.[5]

Many young people are moved often, increasing their isolation and vulnerability to harm. Older children are more likely to experience multiple placement moves in a year than other children

---

4   Reporting year 2020: children looked after in England including adoptions, 2020, Department for Education.

5   Reporting year 2021: looked after children aged 16 to 17 in independent or semi-independent placements, 2022, Department for Education.

in care. In 2018/19, 14% of children in care aged 16+ and 11.5% of children aged 12–15 had two or more placement moves. Those children who were older when entering care were moved at more than double the average rate.[6] Many will also go missing – desperate to get out of their unsafe accommodation or delivering a job for the exploiters who now have full and easy access to them.[7]

These are our most vulnerable young people who are taken into care because they need high levels of protection but are then placed where they know no one, where they feel unsafe, where exploiters can find them and have easy access, where no one is there to protect them – where they are in harm's way. This a recipe for disaster for any teenager and a failure of the care system that is there to protect them.

We hear the consequences of these failures every day. The horror stories are legion.

The teenage boy who was living in a caravan in the middle of nowhere, with no access to family or friends, and having to borrow a mobile phone to call for help. The young people who can't get a suitable care home place anywhere in the country, even though a High Court judge thinks their life is in danger.

The young people who say that they never bother to unpack when they arrive at a new children's home because they know they will soon just be sent on somewhere else. The young people who fall into the clutches of criminals who want to exploit them and know where to find them. Teenagers who fall behind in their education because they've had to move to yet another home and the council hasn't found them a school place months later. The young people who are involved in violence or end up in trouble with the law and in prison.

---

6   Stability index 2020, 2020, Children's Commissioner.
7   Missing persons data report, 2019, UK Missing Persons Unit.

These are not even rare occurrences. Sadly, they are becoming routine.

> I heard of one teenage girl in care who was told to pack her bags and make her own way to a new placement. She had no one to help her so called on her old 'friend' to come and collect her – the person who had been exploiting her. The man drove 100 miles from his home to her house, picked her and her bags up, and dropped her off at her new home before returning home. She knew she could rely on him for help when nobody else would help. He needed her up and running – he needed business continuity. What a shameful indictment of the care system.

We know that there are too many young people who are being failed by the care system in this way. As I told Government when I was Children's Commissioner, while the state can be a great parent, it can also be a really bad one. In fact, sometimes it is so negligent that it would risk having its children taken into care if it were an actual parent.

When the state steps in, it needs to help set young people up for life, not increase their chances of ending up on the streets or in prison.

From start to finish, the system is not identifying teenagers at risk, and even when it does, it is providing a confused and uncoordinated response that leaves some teenagers in an even worse situation. Not only are teenagers not getting the right support, but it is also costing a huge amount of the scarce resources allocated to children's social care.

Without a wholescale dramatic change, outcomes for many children in care will remain poor, and we will not be able to keep some of the most vulnerable teenagers safe. Failing to do so will only build on failure – higher and higher numbers of children in care and ever more money being spent trying to play catch-up as the system crumbles.

Everyone knows that radical changes are needed. The thing is, so many of us also know what is needed.

First, we need to be much better at working out which teenagers are at risk of harm and then be much quicker at responding in a joined-up way.

The data, information, planning, and coordination of response need to be at the forefront of scrutiny by agencies and politicians both nationally and locally.

This is urgent and is vital to both identifying individuals who need protection and finding where the gaps in support are and where resources are needed.

During my time as Children's Commissioner, we estimated that only a quarter of safeguarding boards had an effective way for identifying those children at risk. That meant that most areas didn't know how many teenagers were at risk in their area or have a plan of what to do about it.[8]

Second, we need to prevent teenagers from needing to come into care. Interventions to protect teenagers already being exploited should become a priority. There is no getting away from the fact that the care system hasn't kept up with the changing context of harm that teenagers face. These children are at risk outside the home rather than from within the family – something that wasn't recognised a decade ago in the way it is now. We need to see much better support for young people and their families to keep them safe and out of the care system.

High Court judges estimate that about a third of cases that come to court should have been dealt with through properly

---

8   Keeping kids safe, 2019, Children's Commissioner.

resourced social work rather than a legal case. The system is too risk averse and too quick to take teenagers at risk of exploitation into care. This moves them away from friends and family relationships, instead of working collaboratively with families in crisis. We need to move away from the mindset that it is unusual or high risk to work with the family, and away from the default of moving teenagers into care.

This may explain some of the reasons why professionals are so unsure about new and creative ways to wrap support around families to protect them from those who are seeking to exploit them. One children's services leader told me how she was doing everything she could to keep young people at risk of violence with their families, wrapping the family in support and protection. But she said there weren't many people in her position who were willing to try what was seen to be a risky approach. She knew of only a few others around the country.

How strange that we seem to be missing what is such an obvious way of protecting young people, simply because it doesn't fit in with what has happened before.

Overcautious approaches like these are crying out for creative new approaches to family intervention and support that will help young people stay safe and avoid coming into care, or wraparound protection that works with families by providing intensive support that keeps young people at home with their families.

Where effective programmes are already working, such as No Wrong Door in North Yorkshire, which provides support and accommodation for young people on the edge of care to prevent them coming into care, they should be extended and built upon.

We also have to offer better advice to parents and children who are worried about the threat of grooming and violence and want help to stay safe. National helplines aren't always the answer but every worried parent I've talked to would have really benefited from being able to call a direct line for help if they were worried about their child being exploited. A guarantee of a named person assigned to help and respond would make all the difference.

Third, we need new local care home models that keep young people at their local school and in communities they know where they have support. We must turn the tide on long-distance placements and the shortage and inadequacy of residential accommodation.

There's no more urgent place to start than the thousands of teenagers who are currently being placed in unregulated accommodation. One local authority commissioner told me that when you search their systems for available places for teenagers in care there are almost 50 unregulated places for every care place. That needs drastic action. Government and local authorities need to guarantee teenagers are not placed in inappropriate and dangerous care placements as a basic starting point.

This assessment of risk should also preclude local authorities from placing teenagers in provision in unsafe areas of high violence that have been identified as danger zones by the police. There should also be a pledge to all children in care not to place them out of area unless there is an individual safety requirement to do so. Funding would be needed, but in the long term this will only save funds – reducing reliance on the current homes that, even when inadequate, cost an eye-watering £250,000 on average per place per year.

And fourth, specialist foster carers should be recruited for teenagers at risk. We need people who can understand and engage with young people, and recruiting youth workers to become foster carers would be a great start. The foster system also needs to become much more inclusive and easier to navigate for foster parents from a range of backgrounds.

We need to invest more in black-led services that can work

more closely with the number of black boys on the edge of care and within the system. This should include working with grass-roots black organisations to build a care system that is attuned to specific issues this group of children has and should be part of a targeted drive to close the disproportionality gap in the care system.

Making these changes would transform the way the care system works for young people at risk.

We should be optimistic and remember that we are not starting from scratch and that there are many good ideas being implemented by many charities and local organisations to keep teenagers safe and to boost their life chances.

Some local agencies and partnerships – the police, local authorities, schools, health, Police and Crime Commissioners, Youth Offending Teams, and others – are also developing positive and committed programmes that are making a difference.

We should be looking to build on projects like ADDER (Addiction, Diversion, Disruption, Enforcement and Recovery), an intensive approach to tackling drug misuse that combines targeted policing with enhanced treatment and recovery services. It brings together partners, including the police, local councils, and local health services in areas with high drug dependency problems.

Young ADDER in Blackpool is a multidisciplinary team that supports young people aged 16–25 who are actively involved in substance misuse or at risk of entering the criminal justice system. Each young person is assigned a key worker that they feel they can trust and engage with. This worker will support individuals to address their specific needs, making the most of the wrap-around support available and encouraging young people to take part in sport, learn new skills, meet new people, and improve their health.

The No Wrong Door project in North Yorkshire, which replaces traditional council-run homes with hubs that combine residential care with fostering, is starting to be taken up by local authorities.

The project employs a life coach, a clinical psychologist, speech therapists, and community foster families who work out of the hub, as well as community supported lodging places for 16- and 17-year-olds staffed by specially trained professionals. Every young person is given one key worker, who is supported by a team of trusted and skilled workers – they stick with the young people through thick and thin to access the right services at the right time and in the right place.

The National House Project, established in 2018 as part of phase two of the Department for Education Innovation Programme, puts a small group of care leavers through a 12-month programme of life skills to prepare them to live independently. It supports care leavers to gain confidence and achieve successful independence, secure jobs, and stay in college – often aspirations that have previously felt out of their reach. Those who stick with the project receive their own local authority flat at the end of the programme.

In the London Borough of Camden, the council has developed a Resilient Families programme to drive and underpin the work of the early intervention and prevention services in the local authority area.

Family Group Conferences, mentioned in Chapter 3, are used to help families to be more resilient and prevent them from returning to services. They may address a parental issue or tackle a particular concern for a vulnerable young person, school attendance issues, or behaviour problems in the community. These Family Group Conferences are a way of bringing a family together, helping them to plan and make decisions, and to create a plan to resolve a serious issue. By helping families to address their own issues and create an informal network of support, they build resilience and strengthen relationships.

We should applaud these successes and build on them, taking the best of what is working locally and spreading this good practice across the country. We need a system that is much more flexible, that draws on the strength of family and community, and so supports more children to live with their families and close to the area they know.

The 2021 MacAlister review of children's social care proposed Family Help Teams that would be based in community settings like schools and family hubs – places that children and families know and trust. Before decisions are taken that place children into the care system, the review argues that more must be done to bring family members and friends into decision-making, with a greater emphasis and greater support for kinship carers. Together, these proposals would mean more families could avoid crisis and more young people could get the specialist help they need in the community and, if necessary, in the care system.

The Conservative Government has taken some modest steps to implement some of these changes[9] but there is little commitment or investment to deliver the full programme of reform. The MacAlister review remains highly relevant and vital if very vulnerable young people are to get the protection and support they need to flourish.

Looking at the scale and extreme nature of harm that some teenagers are experiencing in our country, you can only conclude that this is nothing short of a national emergency, which only government has the resources and reach to resolve.

Serious Case Review after Serious Case Review, undertaken

---

9   Stable homes, built on love: implementation strategy and consultation, 2023, Department for Education.

when young people have been harmed, conclude that there needs to be better information sharing with better joint working between the police, social care, health, schools, and the youth justice system. When young people hit crisis, they need to know that all the agencies who can help are doing whatever they can to work together to keep them safe, and we should expect no less.

Despite many good intentions, it seldom happens, and it is so important that I believe it needs to become a legal requirement. A requirement for every area to establish a coordinated, intelligence-led response across all agencies to ensure that teenagers at risk are identified and that agencies work together to deliver a comprehensive and coordinated response.

This kind of local collaboration is vital if we are to keep our vulnerable young people safe, but we should also demand better joined-up working and collaboration across our government and its departments to deliver the kinds of changes that are so clearly needed.

We need a much more coordinated approach within government to keeping vulnerable children safe and enabling them to flourish. Government departments should be working together to establish ministerial taskforces for vulnerable teenagers at risk – in part to continue the work of the now defunct Serious Violence Taskforce that was set up previously.

Government departments love to put people into pigeonholes – those with health, housing, or education problems, or who end up in prison. Life's not like that, and for the vulnerable young people struggling with home, school, their mental health, and the pressure of grooming gangs, nothing is easy or straightforward. There are responsibilities for their wellbeing across Whitehall already, and a ministerial taskforce would make sure they are given priority and focus across government, bringing ministers from all the relevant government departments together in a joint mission – to protect our young people and give them the springboards they need to succeed.

It would take a huge drive of coordinated action to reduce teenage violence and crime initiatives across government, learning what works from the evidence of bodies such as the Youth Endowment Fund and VRUs. It would need to coordinate action around school inclusion, health, and mental health support for teenagers and ensure support is provided for care leavers. It would need to ensure there is the accommodation and the foster carers required for local authorities to provide the right support for vulnerable teenagers in care, and to make sure there is support for their families.

The Treasury would have its role to play, not only by making new money available upfront but also by driving an opportunity and enterprise plan for marginalised teenagers in care to boost skills and employment opportunities. We are letting the talents of thousands of young people slip through our hands, and we will all benefit if we can harness it.

Providing improved intensive interventions for teenagers and their families on the edge of care to enable them to remain safe and with their families would be at the core of such a new deal for children in care, alongside new funding for youth provision in the community, to create safe, exciting, and supporting environments for young people in areas of high risk.

Radical change to our social care system for young people is long overdue and is now urgent. We know what the problems are, and we know what the solutions are. We must conclude that little has changed because there is no driving political will behind making it happen. That is why I push our politicians to commit to delivering better support for vulnerable children and young people and I will continue to do so.

The kinds of proposals set out here and in the sensible

blueprint set out by the MacAlister review are all achievable and would save lives – protecting young people on the edge of care and in care whose lives too often spiral out of control. They would also save money, enabling more to be spent on helping young people stay safe and grow up well. It needs to happen.

CHAPTER 9

Big Ambitions for Young Lives

The young make up 20% of our population and 100% of our future. What happens to young people affects us all. Young people's lives and their childhoods should matter deeply to us – relevant not only to our communities now but also to the kind of society we want in the future.

We don't need professionals and specialists to tell us how the experiences of childhood can impact on adult life. We see it every day. Our relationships, our work, our health, and the way we parent our own children are all affected by what we experienced as we grew up. If we look after our young and support them to succeed, then we all benefit together.

Most children and families in our country are doing well. They receive a good education, they find decent jobs, they will own their own homes, and they can expect to live long and healthy lives. The pandemic and the cost-of-living crisis have had an impact on many, but most will recover. However, there is a sizeable group of young people and families for whom this isn't the case. The impact of entrenched, generational disadvantage and vulnerability is having a devastating impact on many young people's lives, their future opportunities, and our future prosperity.

Many have complex problems – severe mental health conditions, violence in the home, or addictions. These families are most likely to rely on social housing and private renting, more likely to be in insecure employment, and more likely to have health problems and to live shorter lives.

They don't share in the nation's prosperity, and the impact on their children can be far-reaching.

These are the young people who are more likely to start school behind the rest of their peers, begin their education with speech and language problems, fall out of school, and leave school without even the basic qualifications, limiting their opportunities to find good jobs or apprenticeships.

They are more likely to have SEN and more likely to have poor mental and/or physical health. In their late teens, they are more likely to be unemployed and not in training, and they have a higher likelihood of being drawn into crime, exploitation, and serious violence, and of becoming involved in the criminal justice system.

Many of these problems that start in childhood continue into adult life and then cascade from generation to generation without the cycle ever being broken.

The social and economic cost to our country is huge, in not just lost opportunity but also the pressure it puts on public services and the public purse. Too many systems remain unreformed and unable to provide the preventative work that has led to many of the services that are supposed to support vulnerable children surviving in a state of almost-permanent expensive crisis.

The number of children and families in this vulnerable group has grown over recent years and is set to continue growing without reforms to the support and preventative services required to divert them away from crisis point.

Across a typical class of 30 children, six of them are likely to be growing up at risk due to family circumstances.[1]

---

1   Childhood vulnerability in numbers, n.d., Children's Commissioner.

A third of children are growing up in poverty.[2]

One in six children have a probable mental health disorder, rising to one in four for girls over 13.[3]

A fifth of children leave school without the basic qualifications needed.[4]

In England, 200,000 children are vulnerable to involvement in serious violence and 60,000 of these are girls.[5]

The children's social care system is broken, with ever-increasing numbers of children and young people entering a care system that is overstretched and often unable to meet their needs or keep them safe.

There are also significant regional disparities, particularly in the north of England, where the density of more entrenched disadvantage impacts the life chances of many children.

Over the last decade, many of the services and programmes that were put in place to turn these problems around have not been priorities or have been dismantled. Sure Start, dawn-until-dusk schools (which open early in the morning and stay open into the evening after school closes), poverty reduction and elimination targets, a focus on families, youth intervention with teenagers at risk of crime, and youth clubs more generally have reduced dramatically in scale. There has been a 70% cut in spending on early intervention and prevention since 2010.

There is little doubt that the reduction in investment in these services has worsened, at least in part, some of the social problems we are now seeing. All of us can see the impact of child

---

2   Child poverty facts and figures, 2023, Child Poverty Action Group.
3   Survey conducted in July 2020 shows one in six children having a probable mental disorder, 2020, NHS Digital.
4   GCSEs: 100,000 pupils a year leaving 'without basic qualifications', 2019, BBC News.
5   Keeping Girls and Young Women Safe, n.d., Manchester Metropolitan University and Commission on Young Lives.

vulnerability around us – in our classrooms, on our streets, in the terrible news headlines about young people being killed or exploited. Yet this is only the tip of the iceberg. So much remains unseen, happening behind closed doors or in communities that are left behind or marginalised. These children can easily become invisible to those who choose not to look for them, and that includes some of the services you would expect to care for them.

The irony is that the fall in spending and insufficient focus on innovation around prevention has led to higher spending elsewhere. Spending on children's services has rocketed, with many local authorities experiencing serious financial difficulties arising from the eye-watering bills coming from statutory children's social care.

This is financially unsustainable. The 2021 MacAlister review of children's social care estimated that the current annual £10 billion cost to the public purse of children's social care will rise to £15 billion in 10 years unless the system is reformed and £5 billion is invested now on reform. At the same time, schools say they are spending more and more time as 'social workers' because of the social problems in their classrooms. Police chiefs say they spend huge amounts of time and resources dealing with vulnerable children.

It doesn't need to be this way.

Hundreds of thousands of young people are being harmed and held back in our country with devastating impact on their life chances. We need to care about this. This is our society, our young generation, our potential engineers, entrepreneurs, teachers, and health workers of the future. We need to dare to care about it enough to do something about it. As families, neighbours, professionals, young people themselves, and – yes – as voters, we need to choose to value and support our young people.

As other countries have done, we should agree that protecting our vulnerable children and young people is a priority and we should agree that it is the job of our government, in partnership with the many brilliant individuals, innovative organisations, and public services, to help these young people succeed.

We need to be ambitious for all young people. We need to look after our young people, particularly those with the most complex problems and facing the biggest challenges.

We need to understand and tackle the causes of the problems – not just the symptoms that persist and reoccur – and invest in proper long-term help before setbacks become crises and emergencies.

We need to believe in our young people and support and create opportunities for them to succeed. These are young lives with their whole futures ahead of them.

We must make it our mission – part of the way we do things in this country – part of the way we define and see ourselves.

The statistics and the life stories in this book – the relentless loss of opportunity and sometimes the tragic loss of life – demand a different approach. This is why change is so desperately needed.

The good news is we already know from experience and good practice that a bold move to a different approach to supporting children and families is possible. It is happening in some communities and schools right now.

The post-Second World War settlement gave us the Beveridge report, social service provision, our NHS, and the state-funded school system. Politicians understood and made the case for universal services that could support every family and every child to succeed. They set out a new path after the horror and sacrifices of war.

More recently, the governments of Tony Blair and Gordon Brown were not afraid to talk about their ambitions to reduce the inequalities children and their families face, to put renewed focus on helping to balance work and home, and to deliver programmes like Sure Start, alongside a pledge and policies to eliminate child poverty.

Look at the countries in Scandinavia, who top the UNICEF charts for children's wellbeing and life satisfaction. Britain comes a poor 27th on the list, way behind countries like Singapore, Finland, Estonia, New Zealand, and Australia.

If we choose to make children a priority, like these countries so often do, we could bring about generational change. We can transform the lives of the most vulnerable children to break the cycles of vulnerability, of deprivation, of adverse childhood experiences, and of social exclusion, and support them on a positive path in life.

But, as this book has described, we have a long way to go.

If we were in any doubt about how we are doing, the Covid pandemic delivered both judge and jury. In service after service, despite many good intentions and some remarkable achievements by individuals, the system consistently failed many vulnerable children.

Whilst the NHS rainbows on our windows reminded us that as citizens we care for our society and our children and want them to be OK, the pandemic has exposed a system of protection and support that is under-resourced and unable to support all those children who need protection and help.

It exposed the casual way we put children's interests behind opening pubs, and theme parks before schools.

It exposed decision-making systems that are designed for adults but too often overlook the needs of children, and which refused to exempt children in England from the 'rule of six' – the number of people allowed to meet and play – denying children and young people the opportunity of seeing their friends and forcing more damaging isolation.

And it exposed deep inequalities in our society that were only deepened further by young people's experiences during those two years of lockdown and uncertainty – the deep divides between the young people with resilience, strong parental support, and the technology to seamlessly carry on learning online as lockdown hit, and those in overcrowded and sometimes dangerous homes struggling to learn on shared phones.

Safeguarding and mental health referrals plummeted, putting young people at risk and storing up problems for the future. Many vulnerable young people escaped tough home environments as domestic violence soared. Poor parental and young people's mental health rocketed, fuelled by isolation, uncertainty, and anxiety. We emerged from the pandemic with more children and young people with diminished life chances and more young people at risk of those who want to exploit them.

Decisions that were made were often not in young people's best interests and if the UK Covid-19 Inquiry doesn't expose that and look at how different decisions could be taken in the future, we will continue to deprioritise young people if or when any future emergency happens.

We must not forget the disaster that the response to the pandemic and lockdown was for millions of young people or the impact it had on the most vulnerable. It was one of the biggest tests of our infrastructure for children and young people and, sadly, in many ways we failed.

So, this post-pandemic Britain should be a moment where we choose to do things differently. We can start by recognising the scale and nature of child vulnerability in our country and follow that up by committing to bring about change.

As the deep, generational problems in this book show, there has never been a more important time for radical reform and reset of our support for vulnerable children in this country. One that understands the context and the impact of disadvantage, that spots when things are going wrong at the earliest point and is willing and able to respond with coordinated help to prevent problems developing into crises.

It must be a vision that understands how help needs to be built on respectful relationships, that gets alongside young people and families, that goes the distance in their lives, from cradle to career. It must be help that responds to individual needs, that gets to the cause of the problems, and that does whatever it takes to stick with young people and those around them. It must be help that strengthens families and works with them to devise solutions, that believes in people and does all it can to help them succeed.

This is the kind of inspirational support people have been telling me for decades that they need to succeed, and the good news is that, collectively, we do know how to deliver it.

Whichever community you look in, you will find great inspiration in the work going on with young people and families – in schools, in youth centres, in theatres, and on sports pitches. This book is full of examples of dedicated people who are changing lives, often on shoestring budgets and often with little thanks or appreciation from those in power.

There are hundreds of schemes and innovations that are showing us how transformational change can be done, how young people at risk of exploitation or serious violence can be diverted away from it or supported to move on from it on to a better path.

On every one of the visits that I make to these inspirational projects, my thought is always the same: imagine if all young people and families could get this kind of support. Why isn't it already being done, what would it take, and what difference would it make?

We notice these remarkable innovations and become so enthused by them because sadly they are still the exception. Our job will be done when they become unremarkable, and the norm.

To make that happen requires a very different support system for children and families than the one that exists now. It requires bold reform from top to bottom, and a new national mission that brings the engine of government to join with those volunteers, charities, and organisations that are already making a difference, determined to resolve the long-standing social and economic problems at the source of so many of the vulnerabilities we see.

It will take coordinated national commitments from departments across government, backed by the investment needed to deliver the changes required in their areas of responsibility. It would take a strong lead from a single place in government, with clear purpose, milestones, and mechanisms to measure and address when changes are needed.

It would take new national and local coordination and partnerships – understanding that the way change is delivered needs to be dependent on local need but also that a consistency of support is required. It would task and finance local partnerships to undertake vital work on identifying need and ensuring the right long-term response is in place for every different child who needs it.

It would take a focus on the here and now and the challenges and problems children and families face today, but crucially, also an understanding that difficulties often start early and that early intervention from the first months of life, or when problems emerge, is what is needed to prevent those problems from escalating.

And it would take a reconfiguring of how local statutory services work and prioritise their help for the vulnerable – getting ahead of crisis, building trusting relationships, and strengthening and supporting young people and families through long-term help.

If there is one thing I have learned over the last few years, it is the extent of the deep distrust of statutory services that runs deep in many marginalised communities and even amongst families you might describe as affluent and middle class.

So many parents and families feel undermined, discounted, or ignored by the institutions and professionals who are meant to help them. They find that services are unable to respond to their individual situations and so fail them. They are passed from referral and assessment to unattainable threshold to referral without ever really getting any meaningful help.

The system needs to be reset. Our public investments need to start working properly for the most vulnerable children in society, whatever their social background. We need to reform our public services to truly get help to the communities, families, and young people who need it.

This is what could be achieved if those in the corridors of power became ambitious for young people.

I want to see government building a new infrastructure of support for young people and families, and getting tough on the causes of vulnerability – poverty, poor housing, poor mental health, domestic violence, and addiction. It would reshape government finances to provide help from the first weeks of life to support families, identifying if extra help were needed and responding. It would mean ongoing help for families and parenting support throughout a child's school years as children grow up and move towards adulthood.

In education, it would mean an end to the forgotten third of children who leave school without basic levels of qualification and an end to thousands of vulnerable children, excluded or moved out of school, falling through gaps in the education system, which can put them at risk.

It would be a new era of inclusive education that supports all children and young people to succeed by drawing on expert specialist help – mentors, psychologists, and youth workers for children with additional needs or who are struggling.

Schools would be an anchor in the community, surrounded by family workers, working alongside and as part of the Supporting Families' teams and liaising with children's centres, family hubs, and children's services. Buildings would be open from morning to night, opening the resource to the whole community, providing positive and safe places to be, and providing fun, enjoyable activities in spaces where trusted relationships can be built.

It means turning the tide on the profound crisis in children and young people's poor mental health and acknowledging that services are failing to meet demand, that early help is patchy, and that a focus on wellbeing will bring enormous long-term benefits to the whole nation. Let's redesign our schools, our parks, and our communities with that in mind, and ditch much of the over-medicalised, bureaucratic, and outdated system we have now in favour of mental health teams in schools, community drop-in hubs, and 'prescribed' activities.

Government should not be afraid to provide intensive support for families when things get tough. This isn't the nanny state. It is empowering organisations and services to build scaffolding around families wherever and whenever they need it.

Where that isn't possible, and children and young people need to go into care, it should mean better and swifter decisions about their welfare, and a default for children to go into family and kinship care when possible. This would drastically reduce the number of older teenagers at risk from entering care but also put an end to the scandal of the most vulnerable young people being moved around the country and being placed in inappropriate and unsafe accommodation that can put them in danger.

We would have pride in a care system that provides the stability, ambition, and love that our most vulnerable children deserve.

It would mean redefining our country as one that cares for young people and redesigning our public and civic society – from schools, health, and care to the police and justice system – to consider and further children and young people's best interests.

What a difference this would make, not only to the young growing up but to us all.

Devising policies in Whitehall is one thing, but it is the local delivery that will determine their success through new local partnerships to identify need and plan and coordinate services that take on the responsibility – and are held to account – for a new system of support for vulnerable children and young people.

It would also mean rebuilding a vital infrastructure of support for children, young people, and families of children and family centres and hubs.

I've spent the last 30 years listening to families and arguing for and helping to shape the local support they have told me they need. Places to meet, to find support, and to make friends are always at the heart of what they tell me is needed – with trusted professionals there to offer and provide advice and help.

No matter where you go, the response is the same, and those who still have these centres and services on hand are clear about the difference they make to their lives.

The lone parent who was struggling with her own mental health, who felt she would have had to give up her two young children during lockdown if it hadn't been for the support that she received from her local centre workers. The mum who is desperate to escape domestic violence. The parents worried about their children with SEND and desperate for an assessment and support.

The dads who have formed their own support group. The young mum new to the area and struggling with isolation and loneliness who drops into the baby play session.

The parents terrified about keeping their 12-year-old safe after their child has been suspended from school and threatened by a group of boys outside school.

Families who are members of the local community food bank who can get access to good affordable food and can also chat with the volunteers and other families when they are there.

Parents struggling with poor accommodation, with addictions, with their mental health, with poverty, and with debt who can get practical help and professional support to avert or get through a crisis.

Anyone who works in deprived communities knows that these stories are not unusual, and they are part and parcel of the lives of millions of families up and down the land. They also know that this kind of help – once delivered by Sure Start children's centres across the country – is no longer available to a vast majority of families.

Most also know how important it is to replace Sure Start centres and build this vital infrastructure of support back.

A headteacher, weary with his battle with poor attendance and behaviour in school, who finished our meeting by telling me it wouldn't need to be like this if we had children's centres back. The Youth Offending Team manager now just as likely to be working with parents as with young people. The health visitor who can't offer parents with a new premature baby ongoing support because their caseload is too large. The social worker who doesn't have the time or resource to build long-lasting relationships with the children in their care. The school that spends hours each week accompanying parents to the housing office, running parenting courses, and supporting parents with basic food and clothing.

These are all professionals who know that there is a hole in their community where support in the form of children's centres once was before falling foul of a government that seemed so eager to take down what their political opponents had held dear, whatever the consequences might be for vulnerable children and struggling families.

Once seen as underpinning a whole range of government policy areas, it can be hard to remember just how central and high profile the children's centre programme once was.

A multi-billion-pound programme that established what was then seen as a 'new frontier' of the welfare system, a programme that set out to transform the way we support young children and their families, which brought together and coordinated a range of services. At its peak, there were 3,500 children's centres, operating within 'pram pushing' distance of families in the 30% of the most deprived areas of the country and in areas of disadvantage in more affluent areas.

This is the scale of the support that needs to be built now.

After a decade of decline, we now have the emergence of family hubs as a concept, which, although tiny in number, mirror much of the approach of the children's centres that have provided support for children from birth to the age of 19. Most parents won't care very much whether they are called family hubs, Sure Start, or children's centres – they would just like to have one nearby that offers practical long-term support for families to help them with the challenges they face. They want somewhere that offers help with getting decent housing, school admissions, support for a child with SEND, bills, and parenting support, and help to tackle the issues of domestic abuse, addictions, and poor mental health that lie at the heart of so many vulnerable families.

Vitally, they want a system that identifies a vulnerable child's needs early and is there to respond with specialist support, whatever the age of the child. Let's create Sure Starts for teenagers – bringing services together around the school, keeping schools open, providing activities and support – for young people and their parents. Let's put them in all the areas of high violence first and then let's get them to all schools – part and parcel of the way we do things in this country and the way we help our young people to succeed.

As this book makes clear, there is much to build on. Charities like Oasis are enabling families to build stronger communities. Cradle-to-career schools are supporting children to learn as they grow up and progress. Local authorities like Leeds have made it their mission to become a child-friendly city with children and families as a connecting thread throughout their activities and services. In Greater Manchester, they are working strategically to develop an area-wide approach to tackling child vulnerability, while in Southwark, the council is committed to providing accessible mental health support and stopping vulnerable children fall out of school.

Programmes such as the Better Start partnerships in Blackpool, Bradford, Lambeth, Nottingham, and Southend-on-Sea, funded by the National Lottery Community Fund, brought agencies together in a distinct local community to provide better support to families to give their babies and very young children the best possible start in life.

In west London, the Children's Zone is collaborating with partners to support children and young people to reduce the risks of isolation, low attainment in school, unemployment, social isolation, and poor mental and emotional health.

This is the scale and depth of change needed.

The question is always, of course, whether the country can afford to do all of this. It will cost billions of pounds and there is never enough money for everything.

My question is whether we can afford not to do it for much longer. The return we can expect from each one of these investments is a country that doesn't send vulnerable children into the arms of gangsters and criminals, where we are not spending millions on one child in care with extremely high needs because we left it too late to intervene when they were an infant, and where the costs of social failure overwhelm budgets to such an extent that we become trapped in a vicious cycle of social and financial crisis that goes on for generation after generation.

We need a revolution in the way we support young people, and the time to do it is now.

We can transform the lives of vulnerable young people and, with them, society if we wish to.

We need to be relentlessly ambitious for every child.

Index